PERGAMON INTERNATIONAL LIBRARY
of Science, Technology, Engineering and Social Studies

The 1000-volume original paperback library in aid of education,
industrial training and the enjoyment of leisure

Publisher: Robert Maxwell, M.C.

UNDERSTANDING AND TREATING ATTENTION DEFICIT DISORDER

THE PERGAMON TEXTBOOK
INSPECTION COPY SERVICE

An inspection copy of any book published in the Pergamon International Library
will gladly be sent to academic staff without obligation for their consideration for
course adoption or recommendation. Copies may be retained for a period of 60 days
from receipt and returned if not suitable. When a particular title is adopted or
recommended for adoption for class use and the recommendation results in a sale
of 12 or more copies the inspection copy may be retained with our compliments.
The Publishers will be pleased to receive suggestions for revised editions and new
titles to be published in this important international Library.

Pergamon Titles of Related Interest

PSYCHOLOGY PRACTITIONER GUIDEBOOKS

EDITORS
Arnold P. Goldstein, Syracuse University
Leonard Krasner, SUNY at Stony Brook
Sol L. Garfield, Washington University

UNDERSTANDING AND TREATING ATTENTION DEFICIT DISORDER

EDWARD A. KIRBY
LIAM K. GRIMLEY
Indiana State University, Terre Haute

PERGAMON PRESS
New York   Oxford   Beijing   Frankfurt   São Paulo   Sydney   Tokyo   Toronto

Pergamon Press Offices:

U.S.A.	Pergamon Press, Maxwell House, Fairview Park, Elmsford, New York 10523, U.S.A.
U.K.	Pergamon Press, Headington Hill Hall, Oxford OX3 0BW, England
PEOPLE'S REPUBLIC OF CHINA	Pergamon Press, Qianmen Hotel, Beijing, People's Republic of China
FEDERAL REPUBLIC OF GERMANY	Pergamon Press, Hammerweg 6, D-6242 Kronberg, Federal Republic of Germany
BRAZIL	Pergamon Editora, Rua Eça de Queiros, 346, CEP 04011, São Paulo, Brazil
AUSTRALIA	Pergamon Press (Aust.) Pty., P.O. Box 544, Potts Point, NSW 2011, Australia
JAPAN	Pergamon Press, 8th Floor, Matsuoka Central Building, 1-7-1 Nishishinjuku, Shinjuku-ku, Tokyo 160, Japan
CANADA	Pergamon Press Canada, Suite 104, 150 Consumers Road, Willowdale, Ontario M2J 1P9, Canada

First printing 1986

Library of Congress Cataloging in Publication Data

Kirby, Edward A.
　　Understanding and treating attention deficit disorder.

　　(Psychology practitioner guidebooks)
　　Includes index.
　　1. Attention deficit disorders. I. Grimley, Liam K.
II. Title. III. Series.
RJ496.A86K57　1986　　616.89　　86-5014
ISBN 0-08-033134-3
ISBN 0-08-033133-5 (pbk.)

Printed in the United States of America

This book is dedicated to the memory of my father, Dennis M. Kirby, and to my mother Vera, my wife Sandy, and my twin daughters, Molly and Jenny.

E. A. K.

This book is dedicated to the memory of my parents, Dr. Liam and Eileen Grimley, to my wife, Marie, and my two sons, Kevin and Conor.

L. K. G.

Contents

Foreword

A major clinical challenge has been the development of treatment programs for children diagnosed with Attentional Deficit Disorder (ADD). Although the evidence for the therapeutic benefits of medication and behavior modification has been encouraging, a number of investigators have noted the limitations of such efforts (Barkley, 1981; Dulcan, 1985; Whalen & Henker, in press). This is especially evident when one considers the many secondary sequelae (social, academic, self-concept) that may accompany an Attentional Deficit Disorder.

Since its conception there has been much hope and promise that a cognitive behavioral treatment approach would somehow meet this challenge, especially given the nature of the ADD child's difficulties. As Barkley (in press) has recently noted, ADD children suffer from a *rule governed behavioral deficit.*

> What is deficient is the *control exerted over behavior by rules* . . . *the* greatest difficulties are evident in situations where instructions require delayed responding, sustained responding, accuracy of responding, or task-directed activity under circumstances where reinforcement is delayed, infrequent or nonexistent. (p. 24, italics added)

The difficulty that ADD children have in regulating their activities in accordance with externally imposed demands over an extended period of time is most evident in classroom situations. The clinical picture, however, is not all bleak. For example, a number of studies, as reviewed by Barkley (in press) and Douglas (1980), indicate that the ADD child's performance improves when he is asked to: (a) repeat directions, (b) state rules and produce self-directed speech and self-questioning, and (c) pace himself.

Moreover, when the social environment makes rules explicit, makes contingencies immediate and variable, uses back up reinforcers, uses response–cost, programs treatment generalization and makes training part of the naturally occurring environment, sustained treatment effects are much more likely (see Meichenbaum, in press).

Because CBM focuses on nurturing children's self-regulatory skills, the hope has been that it could be used to help ADD children overcome their many difficulties. These clinical objectives turn out to be more difficult and challenging than was first envisioned. Much clinical skill and imaginativeness are required to establish a collaborative relationship with ADD children in order that they can learn the self-control, metacognitive, and social skills required to overcome their difficulties. Moreover, it is now apparent that comprehensive interventions involving family, peers, siblings, and teachers is required. The challenge in meeting these objectives is enough to make clinical-researchers talk to themselves.

Edward Kirby and Liam Grimley have admirably met this challenge and they engagingly share their internal dialogues with the reader. I am pleased to have an opportunity to write this foreword, for I have a high regard for their efforts. Not that it cannot be faulted on some grounds, but rather for what it does achieve. The reader is provided with a mixture of clinical examples and critical-mindedness, clinical tact and sensitivity. The authors are part enthusiast and part critic of CBM, refreshingly honest and insightful about its shortcomings. Throughout, their enthusiasm is appropriately tempered by a recognition of the limitations of CBM.

Most importantly, they deserve a great deal of credit for pioneering ways to program generalization. Sometime ago, Stokes and Baer (1977) admonished us not to lament the fact that we do not obtain treatment generalization and maintenance, but instead encouraged trainers to program such generalization into their training regimens. Kirby and Grimley deserve kudos for demonstrating how this admonition can be translated into specific training efforts. As they note, much more program development and research is required to improve our ability to achieve generalization and maintenance.

The technology for teaching children self-control skills is in its earliest formative stages (see Kendall & Braswell, 1985; Meichenbaum, in press; Meyers & Craighead, 1984). The present book is a welcome addition to this burgeoning literature. As the field of CBM with children develops, we will become more appreciative of what it can and cannot accomplish and where it fits into the clinician's overall armamentarium. The clinical challenge of altering the developmental course of ADD children is still with us. No one clinical procedure or treatment approach is likely to prove adequate. The present book takes us one step further toward that objective.

Donald Meichenbaum
University of Waterloo
Waterloo, Ontario, Canada

Acknowledgements

The numerous research projects that provided much of the material for this book were generously funded by the Fannie and Benjamin Blumberg Endowments and by the Indiana State University Research Committee. Much gratitude is also due to Christy Watts and Vicki McMillen, who transformed pages of barely legible copy into a clean and readable manuscript.

The authors wish to acknowledge with deep gratitude the many helpful comments and suggestions made by Marie Grimley. Her interest in children with attention deficit disorder and hyperactive behavior began during her years as a classroom teacher. More recently, her experiences both as an educational administrator and as a mother provided many valuable insights in the writing of some particular sections of this book.

Finally the authors acknowledge with great appreciation the invaluable assistance of Sandy Kirby. In serving as the editorial consultant to the book, Sandy, who teaches English at Indiana State University, went far beyond the task of copyediting. She labored over each of the many drafts to increase the clarity and readability of the book and in many ways functioned more as a coauthor than as an editor.

PERMISSIONS

Chapter 1

Introduction and Overview

Our beginnings in treating attention deficit disorder (ADD) children can be traced back to the mid 1970s. The inception of our research involvement with this pervasive and somewhat evasive childhood disorder is memorable and was more catalytic than ever imagined at the time. Eight young children were sitting at the foot of a steep staircase in an old house that had been converted into a preschool day-care facility. The teacher's aide was seated on the stairs reading a story aloud. A few children were sitting still, with rapt attention, but most were fidgeting and whispering. One sturdy boy, about 5 years old, was craning his neck to see past the aide and up the stairway. Most of the children were watching him as he squirmed and made room next to himself to scoot around the bottom stair and out of sight. Suddenly, he squealed and jumped up just as water came cascading down the stairs, causing instantaneous chaos as the other children joined his squealing and scrambled over one another, delighted yet wary of this indoor waterfall.

The aide charged up the stairs shouting for me, the senior author, to join her, which I did. The bathroom door at the top of the stairs was slightly ajar but locked. Water flowed steadily from under the door. Jerking on the door, the aide demanded in a stern and loud voice, "D.J. open this door!" Before D.J. had a chance to comply, the latch gave way to reveal a skinny 5-year-old boy with one hand immersed in the overflowing toilet bowl grasping a huge wad of toilet paper and his other hand manning the flush lever. His eyes were wide with excitement. It was only when he saw the approaching aide that D.J. looked around the room and appeared to realize the mess he had caused. During the time the aide was dealing with D.J. and cleaning up the mess, the teacher tried to corral the other children, who were running wildly around the room shoving one another and falling on the soggy carpet. Two boys in the corner of the room were busily consuming the morning's snacks.

This scene marked the beginning of what has come to be called simply *the summer program*. At that time, the summer program involved an arrangement with the staff of this preschool through which advanced school psychology and counseling psychology graduate students applied and evaluated various intervention strategies with designated children. Back then, we did not specialize in a particular type of problem or offer a systematic treatment approach. Many of the children who attended the day-care program were viewed as lagging in maturity and social skills. Although D.J. was their biggest problem, there were several other children who frequently engaged in unpredictable and highly disruptive behaviors. In fact, the staff's plea for assistance particularly concerned the high activity level and low degree of self-control demonstrated by so many of the children.

During the preintervention period, our students recorded baseline data on certain behaviors for selected children. The disruptive behaviors that were recorded included temper tantrums, verbal and physical expressions of anger, and numerous instances in which the staff gave directions or commands that were either ignored, disputed, or disobeyed. These behaviors were highly disruptive to the programs of the preschool; however, in all but a few cases, the children did not appear to be purposefully disruptive. It was, in fact, the lack of purpose and plan that was so noteworthy among these children. Our initial efforts centered around helping the staff better understand and control the children's behavior, and intervention strategies were heavily flavored with behavior-modification tactics. Our staff carried clipboards and stopwatches, recorded baseline behaviors, and targeted specific observable behaviors for change. We talked to the teachers and aides about reinforcement to be applied immediately following desirable behaviors and about ignoring or timing out undesirable behaviors. The graduate students gave signals to the teachers indicating when to apply these procedures and dutifully recorded and graphed the results.

Overall, the results were quite positive. The graph lines generally went in the right directions, and the student-clinicians received, in turn, grateful comments from the preschool staff. We did not do any follow-up studies to see how long changes in the children lasted, but we now strongly suspect that, if we had, the aura of efficacy would have been punctured by the data.

Although this aura of success continued into the second summer program, we had by then critiqued our first effort, and a recurrent question was: Would these children have simply outgrown the troubles or behavior without our intervention? One way of anticipating and overcoming this concern was to shift our focus to older children with a longer or more chronic history of problems similar to those of the preschoolers. Thus, we mailed a letter to all area elementary teachers describing our program as one designed to reduce impulsivity and to increase children's attentiveness and self-control. In response, a number of such older children were referred to our program at Indiana State University. The response to this letter revealed two things. First, there are a lot of children who fit this general description, and, second, such children have a range of behavior styles, making it difficult to establish rote screening criteria.

In order for our program to focus on a somewhat homogeneous group of children, numerous screening and assessment instruments were employed, modified, or designed. These instruments, along with procedures for implementation, are described in chapters 3 and 4. Such criteria foster selection of children who have primary problems involving chronic inattentiveness and who are impulsive and careless in their general problem-solving style.

Children whose poor attention and problem solving appeared to represent secondary rather than primary problems were eliminated from consideration. In this excluded group of children were those who were better suited to the diagnostic categories of childhood aggression or conduct disorder and children with specific learning disabilities involving a particular subject area or a particular mode of learning (i.e., visual or auditory).

In spite of the exclusive, specific criteria for program admission, the number of children referred and accepted becomes larger each summer. The treatment program has come to be increasingly viewed by teachers and other professionals as a specialized resource for certain types of children. We initially referred to these children as hyperactive but now use the designation *attention deficit disorder* (ADD).

ADD children exhibit two major kinds of problems: (a) inability to focus and sustain attention during problem solving and (b) impulsivity (i.e., poor response inhibition) in both academic and social situations. These problems are usually first identified by either the child's teacher or a parent. In the classroom, ADD children often appear to listen badly, to exhibit fidgety behavior, and to work in a manner that is unplanned and sloppy. Particular difficulty is encountered with assignments that require sustained and focused attention. In the home, attentional difficulties and impulsivity are often manifested by the ADD child's failure to follow instructions, disorganization in play and work activities, and difficulty staying with tasks that require planning and investment of effort. A third problem area that characterizes some, but not all,

ADD children is hyperactivity. Hyperactivity is evidenced by such behaviors as excessive running, climbing, and difficulty sitting still.

Previous diagnostic terms that associated such behaviors with some form of brain damage have generally been discarded because no strong evidence was found for a direct link between these behaviors and specific neurological damage. Likewise, the terms *hyperkinetic* and *hyperactive* are gradually being replaced because the motor activity problems these terms emphasize are not always present and are no longer considered a central feature of the disorder in question. The current term, *attention deficit disorder*, used throughout this book, is one that has been gaining wide acceptance among professionals, due to the solid body of research evidence indicating that attentional difficulties appear to underlie other aspects of the problems these children experience.

Returning to our summer program, we continued to employ behavior-modification tactics such as reinforcement, extinction, time out, and modeling. The results of our efforts were quite similar to those reported by other investigators; impressive gains were made by several ADD children on many of the evaluation measures. These gains were not, however, in evidence when the follow-up evaluations were made in late fall. Parents and teachers who had been pleased with improvements phoned us and stated with exasperation that the children were, "up to old tricks again." In our terms, this translated as "back to baseline." The challenge to us then and also to clinicians and researchers is now clear; namely, how to design a treatment that produces durable improvement that generalizes to tasks and situations outside the immediate treatment setting. One may begin by asking why behavior-modification tactics fail to produce durable, and generalized, changes among ADD children. A number of reasons can be offered.

1. If the child responds well to the arrangement of reinforcement and punishment contingencies in the clinic, it would not be surprising for improved behavior to be limited to the clinic unless parents and teachers can effectively implement these same procedures. Though some parents and teachers are readily recruited to assist with treatment, others are not.

2. Focusing intervention on such behaviors as remaining in a seat, refraining from excessive talking, and even looking at the teacher or parent when directions or commands are being given can make the child less disruptive, but one should not expect that increasing such behaviors will necessarily improve the children's problem-solving abilities, learning, performance, and social adjustment.

3. Behavior-modification tactics depend heavily upon the principles of reinforcement. Among normal children, reinforcements can be applied on a continuous schedule during early phases of learning and then faded to a more intermittent schedule later. ADD children, how-

ever, have been repeatedly shown to respond in unusual ways to such a reinforcement schedule. Kinsbourne (1984), for example, has presented evidence that ADD children are underresponsive to reward contingencies. These children require a learning task or event to be compelling in its own right, or else the teacher or clinician must supply external rewards that are concrete, frequent, and salient in order to keep the child involved. Although a well-developed behavior-modification program might include arrangements for reinforcements to be delivered in such a manner, there is additional evidence that ADD children often overrespond to reinforcements and react by being drawn away from the task they are being reinforced for attending to (Douglas, 1984, Douglas & Peters, 1979). Douglas, therefore, agreed with Kinsbourne and with Wender (1971) that reinforcements should be administered consistently and rapidly, but she discouraged the use of highly salient reinforcers. Contingency management procedures can play a part in the overall treatment of ADD children, but a great deal of care needs to be taken in the employment of such procedures. Moreover, the additional sensitivity necessary to successfully use reinforcement tactics with ADD children would need to be used (after specific training) by those outside the clinic if treatment gains were to be transferred and maintained.

As clinicians and researchers were becoming aware of the shortcomings of contingency management procedures with ADD children, a parallel general disenchantment with behavior modification was growing. The principles had been derived largely from work with lower animals and provided a firm scientific base for the psychology of the 1960s, but problems with extending these principles to humans abounded. During the late 1960s, disputes among the various branches of psychology (cognitive, humanistic, psychodynamic, and behavioral) lessened, and a move toward integration of theoretical constructs and treatment procedures began.

In 1977, Donald Meichenbaum published a book titled *Cognitive–Behavior Modification: An Integrative Approach*. In this book, which has since become a classic, Dr. Meichenbaum provided what he described as a "bridge between the clinical concerns of cognitive-semantic therapists (e.g., George Kelly, Jerome Frank, Albert Ellis, Aaron Beck, and Jerome L. Singer) and the technology of behavior therapy" (p. 11). In describing how a cognitive-training procedure such as self-instructional training can be employed in conjunction with traditional behavioral procedures, Meichenbaum also integrated the work of the Russian psychologists Vygotsky (1962) and Luria (1959) into a cognitive–behavior-modification (CBM) approach for children with behavior problems (such as ADD children).

The publication of Meichenbaum's book was followed by an upsurge of studies applying and evaluating the cognitive–behavioral approach. In our own work, we have followed the development of this new approach quite closely. Promising features have been incorporated into our summer programs and evaluated. Because the combined cognitive and behavioral approach appeared to hold promise of producing durable and generalized improvements among ADD children, we were particularly interested in examining studies that reported generalized and/or durable effects.

The following chapters describe a multifaceted program of procedures that are effective in the evaluation and treatment of ADD youngsters. We have derived and developed these procedures with caution and persistence by (a) reviewing the work of those who have experimented with cognitive–behavioral training with ADD children, (b) corresponding and exchanging ideas with many of these individuals, and, most important, (c) evaluating our own experience in redesigning, conducting, and evaluating the summer program each year since 1975. A brief general overview of these chapters follows.

OVERVIEW OF CHAPTERS

Chapter 2 conveys the importance of adopting a broad perspective concerning the nature of attention and describes the cognitive processes and structures involved in the governing of a child's attention during problem solving.

Chapter 3 extends the discussion of attention and attention deficits and provides a description and clinical picture of ADD children. The primary and secondary characteristics of ADD children are listed, and a theoretical model that diagrams the interrelationships between these two groups of characteristics is depicted and discussed. Chapter 3 also addresses the problem of differential diagnosis of ADD children.

Assessment considerations, instruments, and procedures are the topics of chapter 4. Rather than offering the conventional listing and description of the many instruments available, this chapter focuses on measures and procedures that are somewhat uniquely related to either the problems of ADD children or the special requirements of cognitive–behavioral training.

Chapter 5 describes and illustrates the basic ingredients of cognitive–behavioral treatment for ADD children. Step-by-step procedures for conducting self-instructional training in conjunction with a response–cost procedure are delineated. Guidelines for implementation of such cognitive training, along with factors that limit the effectiveness of treatment, are also emphasized.

Social skills deficits have only recently received recognition as a pronounced and pervasive problem among ADD children. Chapter 6 explains our approach to teaching interpersonal problem-solving skills as an aid to improving the social adjustment of these children. In addition, the chapter discusses innovative approaches to the assessment of problem situations, including the thoughts and feelings that occur in these situations and produce dysfunctional behavior.

Chapter 7 relates how the multiple components described in the earlier chapters are combined into our summer treatment program. This final chapter features an evaluation of the generalized and durable effects of one of our recent summer programs.

Lastly, chapter 8 provides an overall summary with some concluding remarks.

GENERAL COMMENTS

After trying several versions of nonsexist language, we decided to refer to ADD children in the masculine because the number of boys diagnosed as ADD outnumbers girls by at least ten to one, and, moreover, a precedent has been set by others who write about ADD children. Also, for brevity and clarity, cognitive–behavioral training is often described simply as *cognitive training*. Unless stated otherwise, *cognitive training*, when used to describe our summer programs, involves the use of behavioral procedures such as response–cost.

Throughout the book, case examples clarify and illustrate various points. The behaviors and verbalizations depicted in these examples were extracted from videotapes; however, the actual names of children have been changed.

Chapter 2

Attention, Cognition, and ADD Children

Chapter 1 described the diagnostic term *attention deficit disorder* as an improvement over previous terms such as *hyperactive* and *hyperkinetic* specifically because the problems of focusing and sustaining attention are, unlike with hyperactivity, virtually always evident among the group of children now described as ADD. This chapter discusses and illustrates the nature of the cognitive, affective, and behavioral variables involved in the act commonly referred to as *paying attention*. Paying attention involves a good deal more than the initial focusing of attention. Furthermore, the notion of an attention deficit can be quite misleading. Two examples featuring Allen, an 8-year-old who was recently referred to our cognitive-training program, will help illuminate the nature of an attention deficit. In the first scene, Allen is taking the Continuous Performance Test (CPT). This test is widely used in research with ADD children and was initially developed to measure brain damage (Rosvold, Mirsky, Sarason, Bransoume, & Beck, 1956).

Allen is seated before a television screen on which single numbers are being presented at 1½-second intervals in random order. He has been instructed to look for a 0 immediately followed by a 1 and to press a buzzer when this combination is noticed. Allen does well on this task for several minutes, but then he begins to squirm in his seat, standing and sitting and becoming increasingly restless. After 3 minutes, he begins complaining to the clinician that the task is boring. While looking at the clinician, he misses a 0 and then appears uncertain how to respond to the 1 on the screen. He decides not to respond, thus making the first of an increasing number of errors. On three occasions, Allen immediately responds to the 0 without waiting for the next number to appear. Each time he does this he says, "whoops," and on one occasion he takes his finger off the buzzer and places it under his other arm. After 6 minutes, Allen begins rubbing his eyes and complains of a headache. He tries to turn off the television, stating, "That's all I can do. I can't do any more of these." He then puts his head on the table and closes his eyes. When the clinician allows the numbers to continue appearing, Allen becomes angry, stating in a loud voice, "I said stop" and holds the buzzer down for several seconds repeatedly until the task is terminated.

Before moving on to the next example, the reader might want to consider what is being measured by the CPT in the example just given. Does Allen have an attention deficit? Does he in fact lack control over his attentional processes? If so, what variables are involved in controlling attention? What role, if any, does motivation play, for example? How about distractability—is this a factor here? Why does Allen become so emotional, angry, and uncooperative? Is this emotional arousal a cause or a result of his poor attention? These and additional questions might be raised in conjunction with the next example. Here Allen is being observed at his school

> Allen has been racing around the playground for 15 minutes during a raucous game of kickball. When the ball is kicked toward him, instead of throwing it to first base, he begins dribbling it and runs toward the nearby basketball court. A boy on the opposing team shouts, "Oh no, there he goes again. What a jerk." Allen is then tackled by several boys and saved from undue damage by the school bell.
>
> Reentering the classroom, Allen is flushed and appears to be in a highly excitable and aroused state. He takes pencil and paper from under his seat and begins to draw furiously what appears to be a truck with enormous tires. Meanwhile, the teacher has distributed mimeographed sheets of arithmetic problems, and the other children settle down to work on them. Allen appears not to have heard the teacher giving directions and looks at the math sheet with an expression of confusion. He waves his hand frantically, and, when the teacher shakes her head, "No," he blurts out, "But I don't know what I'm supposed to do." Reluctantly, and with an expression of exasperation, the teacher approaches Allen and gives him the directions. He begins to work the problems but, after less than a minute, he raises his hand again. When the teacher ignores him, he whispers to the girl in front of him, poking her back with his pencil. She says, "Ouch" loudly, and once again the teacher approaches Allen's desk. She removes him to a seat next to her desk, and, with her almost constant supervision, Allen manages to complete most of the problems.

Given these two examples, one might readily accept that Allen's problems congregate around attention, but what exactly is his problem? Should the clinician postulate a physiological deficit and perhaps seek medication for remediation, or are the relevant variables here more in the realm of psychology and education? In the actual case that Allen represents, both physiological and psychoeducational variables were considered; however, we began treatment prior to seeking a medical solution. Allen was assigned to a group of five boys experiencing similar problems, and cognitive–behavioral training was begun. After several weeks, it became apparent that Allen was not improving. He frequently disrupted the group with behaviors that appeared to be stimulus seeking in nature, and he was unable at the end of each session to summarize what had just been said and done. At this point, the family physician was consulted, and Allen was placed on a mild dosage of stimulant medication.

The effects of medication were quite evident when Allen was given the CPT a second time. He made far fewer errors, and his behavior in the testing situation was dramatically changed. He fidgeted a little and occasionally glanced away from the screen, and he again complained that the task was boring, but he did not evidence the fatigue and low frustration noted earlier.

At school, there was also improvement in Allen's behavior. The teacher described him as much less of a management problem. His parents were quite pleased with the change, describing Allen as almost a different child.

Although it might sound at this point as if Allen's attention deficit had been remedied and his problems solved, major problems continued. Allen gave no evidence of improved learning despite the appearance of better attending skills, and his social adjustment continued to be poor. On the playground and at lunchtime, for example, although Allen appeared calmer, he lacked understanding of and sensitivity to subtle rules that govern behavior in social situations. Allen's mother was eager for him to continue in treatment, stating that, although he was less intense, he still had most of the problems mentioned in the initial referral.

Returning to our initial question concerning the nature of an attention deficit among ADD children, it is clear that, in the case of Allen, something more than stimulant medication is required to enhance learning and social performance. Those who have worked extensively with ADD children have recently begun to refer to a self-regulatory deficit rather than an attention deficit as the basis of many of these children's academic and social difficulties. Self-regulation is a much broader concept than attention in that it involves variables related to focusing attention, problem-solving variables, and motivational variables. Viewing ADD children with these variables in mind, a clinician has a more solid basis for understanding both their academic and social failings.

VARIABLES RELATED TO
FOCUSING ATTENTION

William James, in his famous book *Talks to Teachers on Psychology* (1899), provided an introspective account of the elusive nature of attention. He wrote

> When we are studying an uninteresting subject, if our mind tends to wander, we have to bring back our attention every now and then by using distinct pulses of effort, which revivify the topic for a moment, the mind then running on for a certain number of seconds or minutes with spontaneous interest, until again some intercurrent idea captures it and takes it off. Then the process of voluntary recall must be repeated once more. Voluntary attention, in short, is only a momentary affair. (p. 101)

In James's terms, Allen might be described as lacking or failing to use distinct pulses of effort to guide and direct his attention. In the classroom scene, the teacher supplied these pulses or signals for Allen by repeatedly redirecting him to pay attention. One might ask what the teacher is requesting when she tells Allen to "pay attention to directions" or to "pay attention to the arithmetic problems." Truly, Allen needs a rather extensive pallette of abilities to comply with such seemingly simple commands. He must be able to

- Calm himself down following recess
- Ignore or not respond to extraneous stimuli (not related to the task at hand)
- Discriminate the teacher's voice from other noises and realize by her tone, posture, expressions, and so on when she should be attended to
- Delay gratification, that is, not ask for a drink or a restroom pass and not give in to urges to stretch, scratch, ask a question, and so on
- Arrange the environment to facilitate attention—for example, by covering his ears to screen out interfering noise while attending to a task, by closing his eyes to hear the teacher better, by using a ruler or his finger to keep attention focused on a specific part of a page, and other tactics
- Notice rather immediately when his attention has strayed and redirect it toward the task at hand

For most school-age children, these skills become so overlearned that they are almost automatic, at least in a classroom situation. The skills just listed can be categorized in the three major ways of defining attention suggested by Posner and Boies (1971): selective attention, attentional capacity, and sustained attention.

SELECTIVE ATTENTION

Selective attention concerns a person's ability to respond to the relevant aspects of a task or situation and to ignore or refrain from responding to irrelevant aspects. Though ADD children are frequently *off task* or attending to aspects of the classroom other than the work they are supposed to be doing, there is no solid evidence that such children are more distractible than normal children. Douglas and Peters (1979) have compared the performance of hyperactive children and normal children on a wide variety of tasks using a number of different distracting conditions. The tasks have included tests of reading, arithmetic, coding, form discrimination, tone discrimination, and naming colors of fruit. The distracting conditions included flashing lights, telephone ringing, recorded music, intermittent white noise, human voices, and the physical presence of others. The typical findings of these studies have been that there are either no distraction effects for the ADD group compared with the normal group or that there was a similar distraction effect for both groups. Douglas and Peters suggested that the off-task behaviors of ADD children that are often referred to by teachers as evidence of distractibility could more accurately be described as stimulus-seeking behaviors. (Allen, for example, sought contact and interaction stimulation when he poked the girl.) It could also be that children get off task because they have a reduced attentional capacity.

ATTENTIONAL CAPACITY

Attentional capacity in simplified terms refers to the ability to attend to more than one stimulus at a time. If, for example, on the CPT, Allen had been asked to respond to 0–1, 3–7 and 5–5 combinations simultaneously, this task would have demanded greater attentional capacity. Most learning tasks, by nature, involve multiple stimuli demands. A study reported by Pelham (1981) indicated marked differences between hyperactive and normal children in their performance on experimental tasks designed to measure attentional capacity. In interpreting the results of this study, Pelham suggested that this type of attention, although somewhat distinct, overlaps with and involves some of the same skills as the third type, sustained attention.

SUSTAINED ATTENTION

Sustained attention is involved when an individual must maintain sensitivity to the requirements of a task and stay engaged in it over a period of time. Both the CPT and the arithmetic tasks required this type of attention from Allen. (So does reading a paragraph or, for instance, reading this book.) An understanding of the attentional, cognitive, and motivational aspects of sustained attention is an important prerequisite to understanding the academic and social difficulties of ADD children. Sustained attention has been extensively studied by Douglas and her colleagues, who have systematically examined the learning styles and performance of ADD children on a wide variety of tasks. In examining the facilatory and inhibitory factors required for success on tasks that ADD children have difficulty with, Douglas (1984) concluded

> Although the "facilatory" category encompasses a variety of information-processing and problem-solving skills, they appear to be characterized by a need for good concentration, careful reflection, and an organized, planful approach. Typically a reciprocal requirement for the inhibition of careless or impulsive responding also is present. (p. 152)

The list of attentional variables presented previously as being necessary for Allen's attention to task exemplifies Douglas' description of facilatory and inhibitory behaviors. With the broadening of the definition of attention to include problem-solving skills, additional variables that are involved in the complex task of focusing and sustaining attention over time can be identified. A partial list of such variables follows.

Problem-Solving Variables Related to Sustained Attention

One must be able to

- Understand the task and one's goals before initiating effort
- Be able to realize when understanding of task and goals is deficient or grossly confused
- Generate a plan or strategy for approaching a task or problem
- Make some initial estimate of the feasibility of the plan or strategy prior to using it and generate new strategies if the initial plan seems inadequate
- Monitor progress toward task solution, starting over if necessary
- Break distant goals into more immediate subgoals on tasks requiring long periods of sustained effort
- Engage in means-ends thinking ("If I do this then . . .")
- Estimate time requirements for a task and budget available time
- Cope with being stuck, keeping arousal and emotions from interfering with progress and avoiding negative and catastrophic ideation
- Consult oneself as a resource when stuck (rather than immediately calling for help or quitting) by memory search and retrieval of solutions to past problems

This list of problem-solving variables, in combination with the attentional variables listed earlier, serves to illustrate the complexities involved in responding to the command "pay attention." In addressing the third type of variable involved in sustaining attention, motivation, one gains an increasing sensitivity to these complexities.

MOTIVATIONAL ASPECTS OF PAYING ATTENTION

Teachers and parents often correctly infer that ADD children have motivational difficulties. However, they also might incorrectly infer that such motivational difficulties are *the* primary problem.

In discussing sustained attention problems among hyperactive children, Pelham (1981) has pointed out that, "Many, if not most, hyperactive children are apparently able to sustain attention for a substantial period of time in high-interest situations, such as watching television shows or playing video games" (p. 20). This would appear to indicate that these children are quite capable of sustaining attention when they are interested and simply need to be prompted or perhaps enticed to do likewise on tasks of low interest. Before accepting this as fact, however, one needs to consider the nature of the task demands of these television shows and games that appear to elicit sustained attention. Queries of ADD children and their parents concerning the types of television shows most preferred invariably produce a list of cartoons and high-action, slight-on-plot kinds of shows. Rather than eliciting sustained attention and strategic effort, such viewing could be reinforcing to the child precisely because of the low demand for such skills. Such shows move from incident to incident with little or no connectedness or sequencing. The child can remain cognitively passive and daydream, or he can attend to, and imagine in conjunction with, the show in an intermittent and sporadic manner without interfering with understanding or enjoyment of the show.

It might be more correct, then, to conclude that tasks on which ADD children appear motivated simply do not require sustained strategic effort than to suggest that ADD children can demonstrate good attending and problem-solving skills on some tasks but not on others. The following list suggests some variables related to the motivational component of sustained strategic effort.

Motivational Aspects of the Act of Paying Attention

One must be able to
- Assess the degree to which a task appears solvable
- Decide to commit time and effort to task solution

- Anticipate, picture, and enjoy the anticipation of successful completion of the task
- Provide self-reinforcement for effort and progress toward solution while minimizing or eliminating negative thoughts about oneself
- Respond appropriately to external reinforcement
- Be realistic in expecting external reinforcement and continue working when such reinforcement is delayed or intermittent
- Keep arousal level within bounds rather than being overaroused and diverted by the occurrence of external reinforcement or underaroused and depressed by the nonoccurrence of expected reinforcement

Having explored three aspects of the act that is referred to as paying attention, let us seek an integration of the information presented by returning to our sample ADD child, Allen. Stimulant medication provided some improvement in his attending behavior on the CPT; yet this task does not make heavy demands on the problem-solving components of attention. On more complex tasks, such as those involved in academic and problematic social situations, improvement from medication was minimal. Addressing the subject of the limited value of stimulant medication, Douglas (1984) stated

> As I stressed earlier, I have become convinced that, if we use sufficiently complex tasks, we will find that the children's more basic predispositions have prevented them from building the store of knowledge and sophisticated problem-solving strategies already mastered by peers of similar intellectual capacity. Recent studies in our laboratory assessing complex memory, perceptual search, and problem-solving skills (Ain, 1980; Benezra, 1980; Tant, 1978; Tant & Douglas, 1982) seem to be showing that, even when the children are well motivated, inferior perceptual and conceptual strategies put them at a disadvantage. This is a problem that neither medication nor reinforcement, no matter how effective, can correct, unless there is a concomitant program to develop the missing skills. (p. 156)

WHAT IS DEFICIENT IN ADD CHILDREN?

What then are the missing skills that put ADD children at such a disadvantage? Using the case of Allen as an example, we have suggested that these missing skills involve cognitive skills, such as using one's thoughts to focus and maintain attention and effort during problem solving. The nature of these cognitive skills is described in the literature in terms of cognitive events, cognitive and metacognitive processes, and cognitive structures (Beck, 1976; Meichenbaum, 1977, 1985; Sarason, 1975).

COGNITIVE EVENTS

Cognitive events are automatic thoughts that accompany and influence a person's behavior and feelings. They are often unconscious or preconscious thoughts in the sense that we do not regularly tune in on them or deliberately monitor them. Meichenbaum (1977) has noted that it is only when a routine is interrupted or when a person must exercise choice in novel or uncertain circumstances that one becomes aware of and begins to monitor these automatic thoughts. Although automatic thoughts, once interrupted, become more grammatical, with subject and verb syntax, in their uninterrupted natural state they are more like "telegraphic" messages (Vygotsky, 1962). Normally, automatic thoughts function to provide preconscious linguistic signals or visual images that then play a significant role in the self-regulation of affect and behavior. Because the major academic and social difficulties of ADD children are related to poor self-regulation of attention, affect, and behavior, it is quite relevant to consider the role of automatic thoughts in connection with this disorder.

It was suggested earlier that ADD children might be described in the quaint vernacular of William James as lacking sufficient "pulses of effort" or perhaps as lacking sufficient awareness of and control over such pulses. In the more contemporary language of cognitive psychology, pulses of effort are described as strings of loosely connected self-statements called *internal dialogue*. An attentive and reflective child, as opposed to an inattentive and impulsive one, monitors and controls attention through internal dialogue that relates to defining and clarifying the nature of tasks, generating the means of solution, monitoring progress and errors, and anticipating success. Children who lack skill in the deliberate use of internal dialogue tend to have problems on tasks and in situations requiring sustained effort, self-regulation, and self-control. The cognitive training procedures detailed in upcoming chapters involve an interactive dialogue between clinician and child during which the child is taught to self-instruct, self-monitor, and self-evaluate in a variety of academic and social problem-solving situations.

COGNITIVE AND METACOGNITIVE PROCESSES

Cognitive processes are similar to cognitive events in that they occur below the threshold of cognitive awareness. In describing the nature of cognitive processes, Meichenbaum (1985) wrote

This term refers to the way we automatically or unconsciously process information, including search and storage mechanisms, inferential and retrieval processes. These processes shape mental representations and schemata. Personal knowledge of such cognitive processes and the ability to control them represent metacognition, which provides an interface between that which is normally out of conscious awareness and that which is accessible to assessment, research and training. (p. 7)

One can readily see that cognitive processes such as searching for cues from memory and making inferences and developing strategies are underdeveloped among ADD children when one observes the manner in which these children approach many problems.

Chapter 4 describes a number of tasks, such as matching figures and disembedding hidden figures, that require the cognitive processes of conducting a systematic search and formulating and testing hypotheses. ADD children typically approach such tasks in an impulsive manner and make rapid, incorrect choices involving little effort and minimal attempt at careful selection of the correct answer. Recurrently, as one discusses with an ADD child his failure to engage in cognitive processing or strategic thinking, one is often struck not only by the absence of available strategies but also, in some cases, by the child's lack of awareness that he is capable of learning, devising, and using such strategies.

COGNITIVE STRUCTURES

Cognitive structures have been postulated over the years by both philosophers and psychologists who address questions of how people construct and understand their world. Kelly (1955) described cognitive structures as transparent patterns or templates that a person creates and then uses to keep the world from appearing to be an undifferentiated homogeneity. Meichenbaum (1985) described cognitive structures as follows:

> the term *cognitive structures* refers to the tacit assumptions, beliefs, commitments, and meanings that influence habitual ways of construing oneself and the world. Cognitive structures can be thought of as schemata that are implicit or operate at an unconscious level, are highly independent, and probably are hierarchically arranged. Schemata are mental organizations of experience that influence the way information is processed and the way behavior is organized. Cognitive structures may engender cognitive and affective processes and events and may in turn be developed or modified by ongoing processes and events. (pp. 8–9)

In speculating about the etiology of the basic deficits of the ADD child, it is valid to raise some questions about the development of these cognitive structures. Given the propensity of the ADD child to live in the present moment, without adequate reflection on what just happened or without consideration of what could happen, might this not impede the development of such cognitive structures? Douglas and Peters (1979) have suggested that the relationship between the behavioral pattern of ADD children and the failure to establish complex schemata could be a cyclical one.

> Their inclination against looking and listening carefully or reflecting upon their experiences in a thoughtful manner would impede the establishment of rich, subtle, and complex schemata, which, in turn, would impair the effective deployment of perceptual and cognitive operations, and the cycle would be continuously repeated. (p. 224)

One vital implication for treatment, if the cognitive structures of ADD children are impaired or delayed, is that treatment would need to begin earlier and be more intensive and extensive than would be the case if the cognitive deficits of such children were related solely to cognitive events and processes.

SUMMARY

The attention deficit of ADD children has been discussed in terms of several variables: (a) those involved in the initial focusing of attention, (b) those involved in sustaining attention during problem solving, and (c) those involved in the motivational aspects of attention. The role of cognition in the self-regulation of behavior was discussed, and cognition was described in terms of cognitive events, cognitive and metacognitive processes, and cognitive structures. The brief theoretical overview presented in this chapter provides a background for the next chapter, which presents an emerging clinical portrait of the ADD child.

Chapter 3
Description and Clinical Portrait of ADD Children

The diagnostic term *hyperactive* can conjure up images of children careening about in an energy-charged and reckless manner. The term *attention deficit disorder*, on the other hand, can evoke images of children looking out the window, daydreaming or fiddling with buttons and shoestrings instead of looking at and listening to the teacher. Although the behaviors denoted by these two terms are quite different and can appear unrelated, there is now a good theoretical basis for a unified interpretation. This chapter includes discussion of a theoretical model that shows the relationship between primary and secondary characteristics of ADD. In conjunction with this model the major clinical features of ADD children are listed and discussed, and criteria and procedures for differentiating between ADD and related disorders are given. We begin with two ADD children.

JAMIE

Jamie is a 6-year-old with black hair and lively brown eyes. When referring Jamie for treatment, his teacher wrote

> Jamie speaks louder than the other children in his first-grade classroom and almost always out of turn. Jamie is definitely an inattentive child. It is not that he doesn't attend to what is going on, but that he attends to everything at once. Despite a great deal of individual help, he seems unable to focus his attention for more than a brief time.

Jamie's mother was also perplexed and exasperated by her son's behavior. She reported that

> Jamie just does things without thinking. He has great enthusiasm for life, but instead of participating in our family, he appears to be happening to

it. He is a very active child whose careening, careless play style often results in friction with other children.

Jamie's mother also reported that his behaviors were beginning to threaten the family's cohesiveness. Jamie was no longer allowed in his father's workshop, because he broke things and made his father nervous and often angry. At a school conference, both parents had become considerably upset when the possibility of placing Jamie in a special class had been discussed.

RALPH

The nickname "Tank" is a revealing clue to the behavioral style of Ralph. He is a sandy-haired, overweight but solidly built 10-year-old who approaches all of life head-on. On the referral form where parents are asked to list five recent problem behaviors or concerns, the following behaviors were described:

1. Kicked his brother
2. Broke the wooden ball off the headboard of his bed
3. Ran in the aisle at the supermarket and nearly toppled an elderly man
4. Was kept in detention after school for shoving another child in class
5. Shoved a child in the detention room

Ralph's teacher noted that, although Ralph was involved in frequent altercations, he was not really aggressive by nature but just unable to control his behavior. Ralph's teacher had tried a number of reward systems, but she noted sadly that it was becoming more and more necessary to use punishment.

DEFINITION AND MAJOR
CLINICAL FEATURES

Jamie and Ralph are clearly different children with somewhat unique problems; however, there are also similarities beyond the fact that each is having adjustment problems. The behaviors these two boys exhibit are well described by the definition of hyperactivity offered by Donald Routh (1980) when he referred to ". . . a child's frequent failure to comply in an age-appropriate fashion with situational demands for restrained activity, sustained attention, resistance to distracting influences, and inhibition of impulsive responding" (p. 56). In the most recent version of the *Diagnostic and Statistical Manual of Mental Disorders*—DSM III (American Psychiatric Association, 1980), the term *hyperactive* has been replaced by *Attention Deficit Disorder (ADD)*. The three major features of ADD are inattention, impulsivity, and hyperactivity. The DSM III cites specific examples of behaviors that characterize these three clinical features.

1. Inattention. At least three of the following:

   - Often fails to finish things he or she starts
   - Often doesn't seem to listen
   - Is easily distracted
   - Has difficulty concentrating on schoolwork or other tasks requiring sustained attention
   - Has difficulty sticking to a play activity

2. Impulsivity. At least three of the following:

   - Often acts before thinking
   - Shifts excessively from one activity to another
   - Has difficulty organizing work (this not due to cognitive impairment)
   - Needs a lot of supervision
   - Frequently calls out in class
   - Has difficulty awaiting turn in games or group situations

3. Hyperactivity. At least three of the following:

   - Runs about or climbs on things excessively
   - Has difficulty sitting still or fidgets excessively
   - Has difficulty staying seated
   - Moves about excessively during sleep
   - Is always "on the go" or acts as if "driven by a motor"

Definitions such as Routh's and the listing of specific behaviors such as those included in DSM III provide a basis for deciding who is and who is not a candidate for the ADD diagnostic label. To be useful, however, a diagnosis, must go beyond mere description. How are impulsive, inattentive, and hyperactive behaviors related? Is there a single variable or set of variables relating to all three? Which behaviors are primary and which are secondary? Answers to questions such as these are needed to form a basis for treatment. Virginia Douglas and her colleagues at McGill University and Montreal Children's Hospital have conducted a large number of coordinated studies that have yielded valuable insights and partial answer to such questions. The Douglas model reproduced in Figure 3.1 summarizes a number of findings. In discussing this model, Douglas (1984) stated

> As you can see (in Figure 1), I have postulated that the problems of ADD children develop out of four related predispositions. These include: (1) An unusually strong inclination to seek immediate gratification and/or

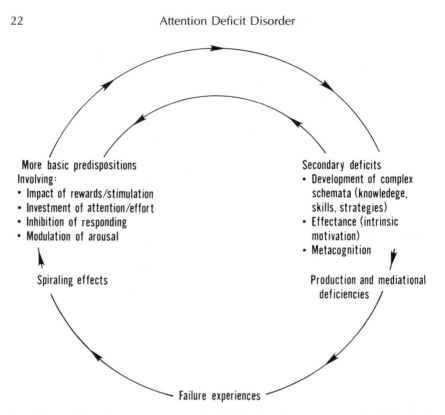

From: The psychological processes implicated in ADD by V. A. Douglas, in *Attention Deficit Disorder: Diagnostic Cognitive and Therapeutic Understanding,* chapter 8, p. 149, edited by L. M. Bloomingdale (1984). New York: Spectrum Publications. Copyright 1984 by Spectrum Publications, Inc. Reproduced by permission.

FIGURE 3.1. Model Depicting Spiraling Effects of Hypothesized Predispositions

stimulation; (2) an unusually weak inclination to invest attention and effort in demanding tasks; (3) an impaired ability to inhibit impulsive responding; and (4) an impaired ability to modulate arousal or alertness to meet situational demands. (pp. 149–150)

Douglas went on to explain that, although she strongly suspected that these predispositions are constitutionally determined, such factors as inconsistent discipline and disordered and confused family life can have a strong influence on the development of the secondary effects depicted in the model.

Of the three secondary deficits, two are quite visible in their effects. These are the failure of ADD children to develop effective cognitive strategies and knowledge, and their low level of intrinsic motivation. An important point to make here is that neither the primary predispositions nor the secondary deficits of the ADD child can be understood in isolation. They are rather intricately interwoven and produce a combined effect. For example, one might speculate that poor intrinsic motivation (a secondary deficit) results in the child's failure to acquire the complex schemata consisting of knowledge, skills, and strategies (another secondary deficit). Or it could be argued that the ADD child's atypical response to reinforcement contingencies results in failure to acquire basic knowledge, skills, and strategies (secondary) in the early stages of learning. This lack of knowledge and skills can then result in school failure and loss of motivation (also secondary). In our experience, it seems more useful to view these deficits as an interrelated outgrowth of the combined effects of the basic predispositions of the ADD child. An example from a recent clinic session illustrates this.

Clinician: Jason what are you doing? You've been just sitting there for five minutes now?

Jason: I don't know how to do this.

Clinician: Ah, you mean you're stuck. Now what did we say to do when we get stuck?

Jason: Use my head?

Clinician: Well, OK, but how do you do that?

Jason: I don't know. Just think about it I guess.

Clincian: Good, let me hear your thoughts. See if you can think your way unstuck.

Jason: What is my problem? The problem is to figure out the chances of rolling two 6's in a row on a die.

Clinician: Good, now what next?

Jason: I don't know. I don't know how to do this problem. (He laughs.) That's my problem.

Clinician: But you have done some problems just like this one. Maybe you can't get this one, but you can at least think about it and get started toward a solution. Remember what we said about making and using strategies?

Jason: Yes, but I don't have any strategy here.

Clincian: Let me get you started by showing you how I use my own thoughts to make strategies and get unstuck. Two 6's, huh. Boy, I don't know; let me picture a die. It only has one six and five other numbers. Right? What did it say in the book? Didn't it say something about figuring out how many of the things you are looking for that are possible and how many other things could happen.

Jason: Oh, yeah, I remember that. I'll try to remember exactly what it said. H'mm, I read that but I can't remember.

Clinician: Stuck again. How might you help your fuzzy memory? There's some important information in that book. Let's see, I remember it was on the left-hand page in the middle, and the rule was written like a fraction with one sentence, a line under it, and another sentence.

Jason: Hey, I can see that! It's about pulling marbles out of a bag. There were two red marbles and three green ones. The picture showed two red marbles, and under them there were two red and three green. That was the answer; 2 out of 5!

Clinician: Very good. Now, how does that help us with the die problem?

Jason: I don't know.
Clinician: Stuck again, huh. C'mon let's generate another strategy for get-
    ting unstuck. We really can solve this problem. Can't we Jason?

Returning now to the point of this example, in observing Jason sitting and doing nothing, we might conclude that he simply lacks motivation. Although it is true that his investment in trying to solve the
problem is low, this is because he doesn't know *how* to invest himself,
in other words, he lacks the knowledge, skills, and strategies that are
vehicles for turning effort into success. The result of these deficits is a
maddeningly passive–dependent learning style that so typifies the ADD
child. Demanding that such a child use his head, think harder, or concentrate will not work if he has no idea how to do these things. The
kind of training illustrated by this example is related to, but does not
fully illuminate, what is meant by the term *metacognition,* which is also
listed by Douglas as a secondary deficit of ADD children.

Metacognition refers to the skill of knowing about and managing one's
own thought processes. A child with a metacognitive deficit not only
lacks strategies for solving problems, but also lacks awareness of the
ways in which one might consult one's own thoughts for some type of
clue or way to get unstuck and move toward a problem solution. In
dealing with such a deficit, metacognitive training involves the clinician's attempts to create or increase awareness and skills in the management of the child's own thoughts.

Jason's response to the clinician's questions suggests that he has both
cognitive mediational and metacognitive mediational difficulties. In
simple terms, he not only fails to use his thoughts to solve problems,
but he also appears unaware that it is possible and necessary to do so.
Some ADD children appear to have cognitive mediational skills but fail
to employ them. Such a problem is described in the Douglas model as
a production deficiency, as opposed to a mediational deficiency. The
following represents an example of a production deficiency

Clinician: OK, Dena, that's the last test item. Now let's look over some
    of the ones you missed. On this one, you were trying to find a chair
    that looks exactly like the one at the top. Show me how you did it.
Dena: Well, I looked at number one and it was too tall. Number 2 looked
    close, so I put my finger on it. Number 3 had shorter legs. Number 4
    looked like the right answer. Five wasn't even close. Six was too wide.
    Then I looked at 2 and 4 and compared each part with the top one
    and I saw 2 had little lines on the seat, so it was 4.
Clinician: That's great, Dena, but you chose 2 on the test! (He laughs.)
    Hey, you showed me a great strategy, but you forgot to use it on the
    test.

Children like Dena appear just lazy or unmotivated, but again, this is an oversimplified and inaccurate description of the problem. A child must not only have mediational skills in his repertoire (such as self-interrogation, self-checking, breaking down problems into manageable steps, and proceeding sequentially) but must also know when and how to employ these strategies and have a sense of competence or efficacy in doing so.

The Douglas model has been helpful to our staff in that it offers insights into the dynamics of ADD children's problems. Focusing narrowly on one or two of the problem areas identified in the model would be unlikely to lead to lasting improvement in overall academic and social adjustment. In many treatment programs, however, this is the case. Stimulant medication, for example, might improve a child's ability to attend; relaxation training and biofeedback might bring about better self-control of arousal level; and behavior modification procedures might increase motivation and investment of effort. Likewise, many classes for learning-disabled children (in which ADD children are often placed) focus primarily on the reduction of failure experiences through lowered expectancy and individual tutoring, whereas the cognitive–behavioral training approach described in the following chapters is a multifaceted approach requiring an appreciation, and at least a partial understanding, of the overall nature of the ADD child's deficits. The word *partial* is used in recognition of the variety of views about, lack of agreement on, and need for further research on almost every aspect of ADD. Despite this variety, there are many positive signs of progress toward a clearer conceptualization of ADD.

Progress in understanding the ADD child is represented by theoretical models such as Douglas', which synthesizes and summarizes a large number of research findings. In addition, it is promising that such a model is in agreement with the findings and interpretations of others who have carried out extensive research on the development of selective attention and the nature of attention deficits (Kinsbourne, 1984; Kinsbourne & Swanson, 1979). This correspondence is even more encouraging when one considers that quite different research strategies are used by the Douglas and the Kinsbourne groups.

Among the secondary problems of ADD children, poor motivation and inadequate learning are the most visible features. These problems, of course, are shared by many children who are not ADD. It is quite important, if treatment is to be effective, to exclude children who resemble but are not good candidates for treatment designed specifically for ADD children. A consideration of criteria commonly used to select children for such treatment will also serve to further clarify the somewhat elusive profile of an ADD child.

SELECTION FACTORS
FOR TREATMENT

Age

In the mid 1970s, when our program was just beginning, we included preschool children in our screening. In one preschool program run by a local housing project, over half of the children appeared well suited to the criteria just described. This amplified our shift from the conventional assumption that early identification and treatment might not be applicable to ADD children, in that most children between ages 2 and 5 are characteristically impulsive, inattentive, and overactive. Backing for this belief comes from Schleifer and his colleagues (1975). They attempted to identify a group of hyperactive preschool children. Two years later, when the children reached school age, only 1 mother out of 20 indicated specific concerns about hyperactivity (Campbell, Schleifer, Weiss, & Perlman, 1977).

Despite difficulties in early identification of ADD children, the retrospective reports of parents quite often indicate that the child was viewed as more difficult than other children from early infancy. Ross and Ross (1976) reported that mothers of children who were diagnosed as hyperactive described these children as being particularly demanding and irritable babies. Sleeping and eating disturbances, frequent crying, and colic were often remembered by their mothers. Other researchers and clinicians have also reported evidence for early difficulties among children subsequently diagnosed as ADD. The reason for discussing this here is to illustrate the point that, although the onset of ADD can coincide with entry into school, it appears that the problem originates much earlier.

ADD children are most often identified and treated during the elementary school years. The clinical myth that persistently accompanies this disorder is that the symptoms diminish or burn out with the onset of puberty. The children in our program who have begun adolescence are clearly not the excited, active children we observed a few years earlier, but they continue to have many problems. It appears that the repeated experience of being unable to fit in and an increased awareness of their difference from other children combine to reduce the intensity and, along with this perhaps, some of the diffuseness of their behavior. A comparison of the Achenbach Child Behavior Checklist profiles (see chapter 4) of younger and older children in our program indicates an increase in the Internalizer Scale of Depression. Depression also accompanies decreases on the Externalizer Scales of Hyperactivity and Aggression. Ross and Ross (1976) have suggested that though activity level of ADD children might decrease during adolescence, attentional, educational, and social difficulties continue, and antisocial or delinquent behavior can appear. The persistence of serious academic and social difficulties into adolescence and young adulthood is well documented (Ackerman, Dykman, & Peters, 1977; Mendelson, Johnson, & Stewart, 1971).

Brain Damage

Historical accounts of hyperactivity or ADD frequently begin with the work of Still (1902), who noticed many of the symptoms we have been discussing (short attention, distractability, etc.) among a group of children who had recently recovered from an outbreak of encephalitis. For the following 60 years, the notion of brain damage and minimal brain damage continued to be associated with the type of disorder currently called ADD. It is now generally agreed that, although brain injury or neurological impairment could well cause some of the characteristics of ADD, an assortment of other unpredictable and varied behavior disorders can also result from brain damage (Rutter, Graham, & Yule, 1970).

A doctoral dissertation (Rumble, 1985) completed in connection with our program looked at the relationship between scores on the Luria–Nebraska Neuropsychological Battery–Children's Revision and several other measures used to identify children as ADD. There were no strong predictive relationships. The lack of evidence for a specific causal link between brain damage and ADD has led most researchers to exclude measures of brain injury when considering children for the ADD category.

Mental Retardation

The behavioral characteristics of ADD are often found among children who are mentally retarded. Mental retardation, like brain damage, is accompanied by a wide variety of additional behavioral characteristics. Therefore mentally retarded children are generally excluded from the classification of ADD. It should be noted here that some of the treatment strategies described in later chapters can be adapted to suit mentally retarded children in cases where ADD characteristics of the mentally retarded child are pronounced and of central concern. There are, in fact, interesting parallels between the work of Ann Brown (1975), who has studied memory processes of mentally retarded children, and the work of those who are developing cognitive and cognitive–behavioral treatments for ADD children. Given the suitability of cognitive training for mentally retarded children who also have many ADD characteristics, a clinician could choose to make both diagnoses. This practice could also be suitable for children who have known brain damage.

CONDUCT DISORDER AND CHILDHOOD AGGRESSION

Harkening back to the examples of Jamie and Ralph, certainly several of the behaviors they exhibited would be called aggressive. Currently there is a lively debate in the professional journals concerning whether or not ADD is really a distinct disorder separate from the diagnostic category Conduct Disorder (Milich, Loney, & Landau, 1982; O'Leary & Steen, 1982; Prinz, Connor, & Wilson, 1981). In one of our own studies (Kirby & Horne, 1982), scores on the Achenbach Child Behavior Checklist Hyperactivity and Aggression scales of ADD children were compared with those of a group of children referred to a family counseling program for aggressive and out-of-control children. Although the family counseling sample was more aggressive and less hyperactive than the ADD sample, the differences were not large. A close consideration of background information for the two groups suggested important differences. Very often, the aggressive children came from chaotic homes where physical punishment was used and aggression appeared to be modeled. The types of aggressive behaviors exhibited by the two groups also appeared qualitatively different. Whereas the family counseling group engaged in anger-based, planned aggressiveness involving power and revenge, the ADD children appeared to engage more often in sporadic unplanned acts of aggression without a strong emotional base. For example Ralph, an ADD child, in discussing the reason for his too-frequent fights, stated, "They call me a name, I just hit them." This was not said with hostility but simply stated matter-of-factly as though no other response were possible.

Prinz et al. (1981) have developed a Daily Behavior Checklist for differentiating between hyperative and aggressive children. The behaviors they believe are descriptive of the two groups are listed next.*

Hyperactive Behaviors	Aggressive Behaviors
Was out of seat during work time on three or more occasions	Hit, kicked, or shoved a child
Spoke out of turn on at least two occasions	Argued in an angry way

---

*From "Hyperactive and aggressive behaviors in childhood: Intertwined dimensions" by R. J. Prinz, P. A. Connor, and C. C. Wilson, 1981, *Journal of Abnormal Psychology, 9*, p. 191. Copyright 1981 by Plenum Publishing. Reproduced by permission.

Tried to get your attention while you were busy with another child

Ran around room during work or quiet

Tapped pencil, clapped, tapped feet, rattled paper on four different occasions

Failed to finish two or more tasks during the day

Asked the same question over and over (four or more times)

Did not listen to instruction and ended up doing different (incorrect) task from other children

Giggled in a silly manner on two different occasions (at a time when other children were not laughing)

Rummaged through shelves or cupboard

Took something away from another child

Made fun of another child in a mean way

Defiantly refused to follow teacher's instruction or command

Threw an object at someone

Destroyed someone else's property

Refused to share something

Forced another child to do something he or she didn't want to do

Cursed

Hit, kicked, or shoved an adult

We have employed the checklist of Prinz and colleagues to exclude children from our program who appear to have more aggressive than ADD characteristics. Although the children we work with do engage in some of the aggressive behaviors listed, they are more likely to commit such acts as shoving or cursing than to hit or kick an adult, make mean fun, or defiantly refuse a teacher's command. The cognitive–behavioral treatment package used in our program includes procedures for teaching the child to monitor and regulate aggressive behavior. The CBM procedures used to reduce aggressiveness work by assisting a child to generate more reflective alternatives and to anticipate the consequences of aggressive behavior. These procedures would be of doubtful value to a truly hostile–aggressive child who knows full well what he is doing and even enjoys it.

CHILDREN WITH SPECIFIC LEARNING DISABILITIES

Children who have difficulty learning (at a level commensurate with their measured intelligence level), which appears related to a specific information-processing problem, are termed *learning disabled* (LD).

Our response to the problem of differentiating between ADD children and LD children has been similar to the way in which we deal with the conduct disorder confusion. Working from the existing literature, and with some commonsense application of clinical impressions, we try to exclude children from our program who would not be likely to benefit from the procedures designed for ADD children or for whom some alternative type of treatment might be preferable.

Douglas and Peters (1979) presented a contrasting model for the development of learning disabilities. For these children, the basic predisposition is toward a specific learning disability such as language or auditory processing. This predisposition results directly in failure and consequent avoidance of learning behaviors, followed by pseudo or secondary problems of distractability, inattention, restlessness, and impulsivity.

The important point to be made here is that, although learning disabled children share many of the symptoms of the ADD child, a treatment program focusing on symptoms that are only secondarily related to the basic problems of an LD child could not be expected to be all that effective unless it was used in combination with procedures for dealing with the primary problem. Chapter 4 describes some of the assessment procedures we use in our program to provide information for differentiating between ADD and LD. Following Douglas and Peters's suggestion that parents be queried as to the preschool behaviors of the child has also yielded useful information in that the predispositions for ADD are often noticed at an early age, whereas the predispositions for LD would not be expected to show up until formal schooling begins.

THE EMERGING CLINICAL
PORTRAIT OF THE ADD CHILD

From a synthesis of the information presented in this chapter, a general pattern or clinical portrait of the ADD child begins to emerge. Shortly after birth, the child is variant from other infants in the areas of arousal modulation, inhibitory control, and attentional controls. The earliest clues to these difficulties might be reflected in the child's response to attempts to schedule his feeding and sleeping. Later, as a preschooler, the child might be somewhat excitable and impulsive and less prone to respond in a predicted way to rewards and other methods of controlling his behavior. These tendencies are usually not alarming to parents or teachers who know that preschool-age children are naturally a bit unruly and unpredictable.

By the time the child enters preschool and Sunday school programs, some concerns often arise about behaviors, but because the demands for self-control and sustained investment of effort in learning are not too pronounced in these settings, the ADD child can escape notice. Kindergarten and first grade, however, usually present a major set of obstacles to a child with ADD tendencies. The child's sporadic and uneven periods of attending while the basic rules for decoding our language, spelling, and arithmetic are being taught result in poor learning and performance in school. Assignments are skipped, not completed, done in a messy way, and are often wrong. Directions for seatwork and other projects are missed, misunderstood, or ignored. Lack of success in school and negative feedback urge the child to abandon further effort. Already, he begins to look around for ways of making the dull and frustrating routine of school more interesting (thus making himself miss even more crucially instructive matter). And the vicious circle is spinning.

One way to keep school interesting and tolerable, which fits the ADD child's predispositions, is to become the class clown or perhaps the class bully. Or a child might just become intensely social. Other children enjoy the freshness and unpredictableness of the ADD child at first, but the same predispositions that cause academic failure lead eventually to social adjustment problems as well.

The cumulative effects of failure, punishment, rejection, and just not fitting in take their toll, and the 12- or 13-year-old ADD child begins to show the distressing signs of these experiences. Some abatement of symptoms often occurs with adulthood, if a vocation is found that reduces the demands for abilities and skills that are lacking. But the prognosis for an untreated ADD child is generally not a happy one; contact with mental health and criminal justice agencies, marriage problems, and multiple job changes are a familiar pattern.

To end this chapter on a note of optimism, though, it should be stated that the intense research activity concerning almost every aspect of ADD in recent years is beginning to pay off. There are several signs of encouragement, as researchers and clinicians combine efforts to identify, understand, and treat ADD children. As techniques are refined, more ADD children will be identified and at least partially remediated. Those who have worked with ADD children for a number of years are now coming to agree that short-term treatments aimed at one or two of the more salient aspects of this childhood disorder do not work. What is needed is a treatment package that addresses the complexity and pervasiveness of the problem. The following chapters describe some beginnings in the development of such a treatment package.

Chapter 4

Assessment

Chapter 1 explained how our summer program grew from a behavioral treatment program into a cognitive–behavioral one. The difference that this shift entails is perhaps nowhere better illustrated than in the kinds of assessment instruments and procedures that have been incorporated into the program during the past several years. Cognitive–behavioral assessment calls for measures that provide sensitive and meaningful information concerning not only the child's behavior but also the thoughts and feelings that precede and accompany behavior. Information gained from assessment is used to (a) select children appropriate for treatment, (b) identify target behaviors for treatment, and (c) monitor and evaluate effects of treatment. A thorough approach to assessment is directed at both the molar and molecular levels of behavior and is guided by consideration of the child's strengths and weaknesses.

Given these considerations in conjunction with the heterogeneity of the problems ADD children exhibit (inattention, impulsivity, poorly modulated arousal, low achievement, low self-esteem, inadequate social skills, etc.), it should not be surprising that a multifaceted assessment approach is needed. The purpose of this chapter is to guide the reader through the assessment procedures currently used in our treatment program. Where space permits, samples of the instruments that have been developed, modified, and employed will be illustrated, along with descriptive data obtained from a recent sample of 23 ADD children. We begin with the parents as an important source of assessment data.

PARENTS AS AN INFORMATION SOURCE

Parents were described by Whalen and Henker (1980) as ". . . a rich and often untapped source about atypical child development and family coping strategies" (p. 348). They went on to say that, although it is true that information provided by parents is often misleading and im-perfect, such criticism can also be leveled at most other sources, even those considered standardized and highly objective, such as teacher checklists and even physiological recording devices. Among the factors that could cause parent information to be inaccurate are (a) low edu-cation and/or intelligence level, (b) limited experience in completing rating scales and questionnaires, (c) lack of knowledge concerning age-appropriate or normative behavior (sometimes exemplified by parents of first or only children) and (d) lack of time or perhaps lack of aware-ness of the importance of information obtained through case history forms, rating scales, and questionnaires mailed to parents or completed in the clinic waiting room. One way to minimize the inaccuracies stem-ming from these sources is to collect parent data in the context of a personal interview.

PARENT INTERVIEW

Part one of the parent interview used in our program is shown in Figure 4.1. The questions concerning the child's behavior during early infancy and childhood were derived from studies showing that the ac-ademic and social difficulties of the school-age ADD child can quite often be traced to much earlier signs of atypical development. Among these early indicators of ADD tendencies are scheduling problems, sen-sitivity to noise, high general activity level, and lack of persistence and concentration.

The second part of the parent interview (Figure 4.2) consists of the list of symptoms or behavioral characteristics of ADD children. This list is from the Diagnostic and Statistical Manual—DSM III and was altered by Pelham, Atkins, Murphy, and White (1981) into a checklist for par-ents or teachers. Depending upon the clinician's impression of the par-ent, these items may be read to the parent or the parent may be asked to reflect upon and rate his or her child on each item. Norms for boys and girls in grades K–5 were also collected by Pelham and are also presented in Figure 4.2.

Part three of the parent interview (Figure 4.3) is a slightly altered form of the Home Situations Questionnaire (HSQ) developed by Bark-ley (1981). On Barkley's original questionnaire, parents rated each sit-uation, using a 9-point scale, with a 1 being *mild* and a 9 being *severe*. This was altered to a 3-choice scale to reduce the complexity and to allow more direct comparison with the Conners Parent Symptom Questionnaire. As with the DSM questionnaire, the clinician may read the HSQ aloud or have the parents read it thoughtfully on their own. Even in cases in which parents are judged competent to complete these

FIGURE 4.1. Parent Interview Form for ADD Program

PART 1

Permission to tape record   Video _____ Audio _____

Child's Name _____ Birthday _____ Age _____

Address _____ Home Phone _____

School _____ Grade ____ Teacher _____

Family Physician _____

Previous professional assistance for child's
  problem   Yes ____ No ____

Previous medication related to current problem.   Yes ____ No ____

If yes, give name _____ Dosage _____

How long _____ Continuous or summer off _____

Current state of medication _____

Parent opinion of medication effects.

Brief look at developmental history as it may relate to current problems:
  Anything unusual about pregnancy or birth?
  Any trauma, head injury, etc.?
  Age when problem began and brief description.
  Sleeping or eating problems? Describe.

  General
  Describe what the child was like during infancy.

  Probe
  Scheduling problems
  Sensitivity to noise
  Reaction to change
  Activity level

  General
  Describe early childhood.

  Probe
  Persistence
  Concentration
  Activity level
  Moodiness
  Going along with others

FIGURE 4.2. SNAP Checklist and Total Score Norms for the SNAP Checklist

Child's Name: _____ Age: ____ Grade: ____ Sex: ____

Completed by: Mother ____ Father ____ Teacher ____ Other ____

OBSERVATION	Not at all	Just a little	Pretty much	Very much
Hyperactivity				
1. Excessive running or climbing				
2. Difficulty sitting still or excessive fidgeting				
3. Difficulty staying seated				
4. Motor restlessness during sleep (Parents) Motor restlessness (Teacher)				
5. Always on the go or acts as if "driven by a motor"				
Inattention				
1. Often fails to finish things he or she starts				
2. Often doesn't seem to listen				
3. Easily distracted				
4. Difficulty sticking to a play activity				
5. Difficulty concentrating on school work or other tasks requiring sustained attention				
Impulsivity				
1. Often acts before thinking				
2. Excessive shifting from one activity to another				
3. Has difficulty organizing work (not due to cognitive impairment)				
4. Needs a lot of supervision				

FIGURE 4.2. *(continued)*

	Not at all	Just a little	Pretty much	Very much
5. Frequent calling out in class				
6. Difficulty waiting for turn in games or group situations				
Peer Interactions 1. Fights, hits, punches, etc				
2. Is disliked by other children				
3. Frequently interrupts other children's activities				
4. Bossy; always telling other children what to do				
5. Teases or calls other children names				
6. Refuses to participate in group activities				

Total score norms for the SNAP checklist

Grade	Boys Mean	s.d.	Girls Mean	s.d.	N Boys	Girls
k–1	15.7	12.3	10.6	9.4	91	99
2–3	12.6	13.4	5.7	10.0	101	99
4–5	9.0	10.3	5.4	8.6	105	113

Note: Four teachers at each grade level (24 teachers total) rated their entire classes to generate these norms. It should be noted that the distributions are skewed. The modal total score is zero.

From: Operationalization and validation of attention deficit disorder by W. E. Pelham, M. S. Atkins, H. A. Murphy, and K. S. White, 1981. Paper presented at the annual meeting of the Association for Advancement of Behavioral Therapy, Toronto, November 1981. Reproduced by permission.

measures on their own, information can be gained from presenting these items orally and in a conversational manner. In addition to obtaining information from parents in the initial interview, the clinician is also judging parental willingness and ability to participate in treatment. Later this will become critical to treatment and generalization.

FIGURE 4.3. Home Situations Questionnaire (HSQ)

Name of child: _____

Name of respondent/relation: _____

Does this child present any behavior problems in any of these situations? Please circle your answers.

	Yes/No	If yes, how much are they a problem?		
		Just a Little	Pretty Much	Very Much
Playing alone	Yes No	★	★	★
Playing with other children	Yes No	★	★	★
At meals	Yes No	★	★	★
Getting dressed	Yes No	★	★	★
Washing/bathing	Yes No	★	★	★
When you are on the telephone	Yes No	★	★	★
Watching TV	Yes No	★	★	★
When visitors are in your home	Yes No	★	★	★
When you are visiting someone else	Yes No	★	★	★
When in stores, supermarkets, church, restaurants, or other public places	Yes No	★	★	★
When asked to do chores at home	Yes No	★	★	★
Going to bed	Yes No	★	★	★
In the car	Yes No	★	★	★
When with a babysitter	Yes No	★	★	★
At school	Yes No	★	★	★
When asked to do school homework	Yes No	★	★	★

From: Hyperactive Children: A Handbook for Diagnosis and Treatment by R. A. Barkley, 1981, New York: Guilford Press. Copyright 1981 by Guilford Press. Adapted by permission.

QUESTIONNAIRES AND RATING SCALES

The most widely used and carefully researched parent rating scale is the Parent Symptom Questionnaire (PSQ) developed by C. Keith Conners (1969). The 48-item version of this questionnaire (see Figure 4.4) includes 10 items that are scored for hyperactivity. A factor analytic study of the PSQ by Goyette, Conners, and Ulrich (1978) yielded the following five factors: inattention–learning problems, aggression–conduct problems, impulsivity–hyperactivity problems, psychosomatic problems, and anxiety problems.

FIGURE 4.4. Parent Symptom Questionnaire (PSQ)

Name of Child _____ Date _____

Please answer all questions. Beside each item below, indicate the degree of the problem by a check mark (√)	Not at all	Just a little	Pretty much	Very much
1. Picks at things (nails, fingers, hair, clothing)				
2. Sassy to grown-ups				
3. Problems with making or keeping friends				
4. Excitable, impulsive				
5. Wants to run things				
6. Sucks or chews (thumb, clothing, blankets)				
7. Cries easily or often				
8. Carries a chip on shoulder				
9. Daydreams				
10. Difficulty in learning				
11. Restless in the "squirmy" sense				
12. Fearful (of new situations, new people or places, going to school)				

FIGURE 4.4. (*continued*)

13. Restless, always up and on the go					
14. Destructive					
15. Tells lies or stories that aren't true					
16. Shy					
17. Gets into more trouble than others same age					
18. Speaks differently from others same age (baby talk, stuttering, hard to understand)					
19. Denies mistakes or blames others					
20. Quarrelsome					
21. Pouts and sulks					
22. Steals					
23. Disobedient or obeys resentfully					
24. Worries more than others (about being alone; illness or death)					
25. Fails to finish things					
26. Feelings easily hurt					
27. Bullies others					
28. Unable to stop a repetitive activity					
29. Cruel					
30. Childish or immature (wants help he shouldn't need; clings; needs constant reassurance)					
31. Distractibility or attention span a problem					
32. Headaches					
33. Mood changes quickly and drastically					

FIGURE 4.4. (*continued*)

	Not at all	Just a little	Pretty much	Very much
34. Doesn't like or doesn't follow rules or restrictions				
35. Fights constantly				
36. Doesn't get along well with brothers or sisters				
37. Easily frustrated in efforts				
38. Disturbs other children				
39. Basically an unhappy child				
40. Problems with eating (poor appetite; up between bites)				
41. Stomachaches				
42. Problems with sleep (can't fall asleep, up too early, up in the night)				
43. Other aches and pains				
44. Vomiting or nausea				
45. Feels cheated in family circle				
46. Boasts and brags				
47. Lets self be pushed around				
48. Bowel problems (frequently loose, irregular habits, constipation)				

Reproduced by permission of the author.

Our experience with the PSQ indicated that, despite some limitations, it is useful as an initial screening measure. The generally recommended cutoff score of 1.5 tends to result in a higher number of children being selected for treatment than most prevalence estimates of ADD would predict (Kendall & Braswell, 1985). Among these children are ones who are more accurately described by designations such as aggressive child syndrome or conduct disorder. A score of two standard deviations or more above the mean for the child's age group is likely to provide a more realistic screening criterion. Another point worth noting is that ADD children who score high on the PSQ anxiety scale (items 12, 16, 24, 47) have been found to respond less well to stimulant medication than lower scoring children (Barkley, 1981). This finding suggests that anxious ADD children might represent a subgroup.

SELF-CONTROL RATING SCALE (SCRS)

The SCRS is a 33-item scale developed by Kendall and Wilcox (1979). This scale (shown in Figure 4.5) contains items relating to the child's self-control, impulsivity, and a combination of these two variables. Using a 7-point scale, the parent indicates the degree to which each item characterizes the child (e.g., $1 = always$; $7 = never$). The SCRS has been shown to be related to classroom behavior (Kendall, Zupan, & Braswell, 1981) and to be sensitive to changes produced by cognitive–behavioral treatment (Kendall & Wilcox, 1980). With regard to identification of specific groups of children, hyperactive children were found to obtain a higher mean score ($x = 170$) than conduct disorder children ($x = 148$) or children with internalizing types of problems ($x = 137$) such as fears or somatic disorders (Robin, Fischel, & Brown, 1984). In addition to aiding the clinician in the identification of ADD children and in the evaluation of treatment effects, the items on the SCRS lend themselves well to one of the major goals of assessment, namely, identification of specific target areas for treatment. Instead of designing a generalized self-control treatment package, the clinician can select for initial treatment those items that have the highest ratings for an individual ADD child.

TEACHER RATING SCALE (TRS)

The TRS (Figure 4.6) is a 39-item scale developed by C. Keith Conners (1969) that is similar in format to the PSQ. It is the most widely used and most fully researched teacher rating scale for ADD available. As with the PSQ, this scale tends to include not only children who have attention deficit disorders but also those who are disruptive and noncompliant. It is possible to deal with this limitation of the scale by treating the TRS as an initial screening device with a cutoff score of 1.5 or higher on the hyperactivity scale. Other measures, such as the Daily

FIGURE 4.5. Self-control Rating Scale (SCRS)

Name of Child _____ Grade _____

Rater _____ Date _____

Please rate this child according to the descriptions below by circling the appropriate number. The underlined 4 in the center of each row represents where the average child would fall on this item. Please do not hesitate to use the entire range of possible ratings.

1. When the child promises to do something, can you count on him or her to do it?

1	2	3	4	5	6	7
always						never

2. Does the child butt into games or activities even when he or she hasn't been invited?

1	2	3	4	5	6	7
never						often

3. Can the child deliberately calm down when he or she is excited or all wound up?

1	2	3	4	5	6	7
yes						no

4. Is the quality of the child's work all about the same or does it vary a lot?

1	2	3	4	5	6	7
same						varies

5. Does the child work for long-range goals?

1	2	3	4	5	6	7
yes						no

6. When the child asks a question, does he or she wait for an answer, or jump to something else (e.g., a new question) before waiting for an answer?

1	2	3	4	5	6	7
waits						jumps

7. Does the child interrupt inappropriately in conversations with peers, or wait his or her turn to speak?

1	2	3	4	5	6	7
waits						interrupts

8. Does the child stick to what he or she is doing until he or she is finished with it?

1	2	3	4	5	6	7
yes						no

9. Does the child follow the instructions of responsible adults?

1	2	3	4	5	6	7
always						never

10. Does the child have to have everything right away?

1	2	3	4	5	6	7
no						yes

11. When the child has to wait in line, does he or she do so patiently?

1	2	3	4	5	6	7
yes						no

12. Does the child sit still?

1	2	3	4	5	6	7
yes						no

13. Can the child follow suggestions of others in group projects, or does he or she insist on imposing his or her own ideas?

1	2	3	4	5	6	7
able to follow						imposes

FIGURE 4.5. (*continued*)

14. Does the child have to be reminded several times to do something before he or she does it?

1 2 3 <u>4</u> 5 6 7
never   always

15. When reprimanded, does the child answer back inappropriately?

1 2 3 <u>4</u> 5 6 7
never   always

16. Is the child accident-prone?

1 2 3 <u>4</u> 5 6 7
no   yes

17. Does the child neglect or forget regular chores or tasks?

1 2 3 <u>4</u> 5 6 7
never   always

18. Are there days when the child seems incapable of settling down to work?

1 2 3 <u>4</u> 5 6 7
never   often

19. Would the child more likely grab a smaller toy today or wait for a larger toy tomorrow, if given the choice?

1 2 3 <u>4</u> 5 6 7
wait   grab

20. Does the child grab for the belongings of others?

1 2 3 <u>4</u> 5 6 7
never   often

21. Does the child bother others when they're trying to do things?

1 2 3 <u>4</u> 5 6 7
no   yes

22. Does the child break basic rules?

1 2 3 <u>4</u> 5 6 7
never   always

23. Does the child watch where he or she is going?

1 2 3 <u>4</u> 5 6 7
always   never

24. In answering questions, does the child give one thoughtful answer, or blurt out several answers all at once?

1 2 3 <u>4</u> 5 6 7
one answer   several

25. Is the child easily distracted from his or her work or chores?

1 2 3 <u>4</u> 5 6 7
no   yes

26. Would you describe this child more as careful or careless?

1 2 3 <u>4</u> 5 6 7
careful   careless

27. Does the child play well with peers (follows rules, waits turn, cooperates)?

1 2 3 <u>4</u> 5 6 7
yes   no

28. Does the child jump or switch from activity to activity rather than sticking to one thing at a time?

1 2 3 <u>4</u> 5 6 7
sticks to one   switches

29. If a task is at first too difficult for the child, will he or she get frustrated and quit, or first seek help with the problem?

1 2 3 <u>4</u> 5 6 7
seek help   quit

30. Does the child disrupt games?

1 2 3 <u>4</u> 5 6 7
never   often

31. Does the child think before he or she acts?

1 2 3 <u>4</u> 5 6 7
always   never

FIGURE 4.5. (*continued*)

32. If the child payed more attention to his or her work, do you think he or she would do much better than at present?

   1   2   3   <u>4</u>   5   6   7
   no   yes

33. Does the child do too many things at once, or does he or she concentrate on one thing at a time?

   1   2   3   <u>4</u>   5   6   7
   one thing   too many

List five or six *specific* examples of impulsive and/or inattentive behaviors your child has shown at home *in the last week:*

1.

2.

3.

4.

5.

6.

Behavior Checklist, described in chapter 3, can then be used to identify those children with highly aggressive behaviors who require alternative treatments.

CHILD BEHAVIOR CHECKLIST (CBCL)

The CBCL, developed by Thomas Achenbach (1978), consists of 113 items describing a wide variety of problems experienced by elementary school children (see Figure 4.7). The parent indicates whether each item is *very true* (score of 2), *somewhat true* (score of 1), or *not true* (score of 0). The results can be computer scored and profiled using a program

FIGURE 4.6. Teacher Rating Scale (TRS)

Date _____ Name of child _____

TEACHER'S QUESTIONNAIRE

Listed below are descriptive terms of behavior. Place a check mark in the column which best describes the child. ANSWER ALL ITEMS.

	Degree of Activity			
OBSERVATION	Not at all	Just a little	Pretty much	Very much
Classroom Behavior				
1. Constantly fidgeting				
2. Hums and makes other odd noises				
3. Demands must be met immediately—easily frustrated				
4. Coordination poor				
5. Restless or overactive				
6. Excitable, impulsive				
7. Inattentive, easily distracted				
8. Fails to finish things he starts— short attention span				
9. Overly sensitive				
10. Overly serious or sad				
11. Daydreams				
12. Sullen or sulky				
13. Cries often and easily				
14. Disturbs other children				
15. Quarrelsome				
16. Mood changes quickly and drastically				

FIGURE 4.6. (*continued*)

	Not at all	Just a little	Pretty much	Very much
17. Acts "smart"				
18. Destructive				
19. Steals				
20. Lies				
21. Temper outburst, explosive and unpredictable behavior				
Group Participation				
22. Isolates himself or herself from other children				
23. Appears to be unaccepted by group				
24. Appears to be easily led				
25. No sense of fair play				
26. Appears to lack leadership				
27. Does not get along with opposite sex				
28. Does not get along with same sex				
29. Teases other children or interferes with their activities				
Attitude Toward Authority				
30. Submissive				
31. Defiant				
32. Impudent				
33. Shy				
34. Fearful				
35. Excessive demands for teacher's attention				

FIGURE 4.6. (*continued*)

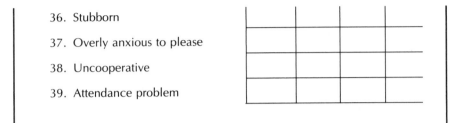

36. Stubborn

37. Overly anxious to please

38. Uncooperative

39. Attendance problem

Reproduced by permission of the author.

and norms developed by Achenbach, which allows the clinician to compare a particular child's score with the scores of a large sample of normal children and with the scores for a sample of children referred to mental health centers across the country for various adjustment problems. Figure 4.8 shows the profile of our ADD sample on the CBCL.

CHILD INTERVIEW

As with the parent interview, the child interview was designed with sensitivity to the uniqueness of ADD children. It consists of four parts.

Part I: Child's Perception of the Problem
Goal. To obtain information and form hypotheses concerning the child's own perception of his problem and reason for being in the program.

Rationale. Cognitive–behavioral treatment requires the full active involvement of the child. Children who are either quite negative about being in treatment or confused, uninformed, or passive about treatment do not respond well. This does not mean that only children who are aware of their problem and eager to cooperate will be accepted. It is important, however, for the clinician to be aware of the child's perceptions of his problem and the reasons for his being referred for treatment. The clinician can then anticipate the extent to which these perceptions will facilitate or interfere with treatment goals.

General Interview Questions

1. How are things going at school? (Probe) Any particular problems this week?

FIGURE 4.7. Child Behavior Checklist for Ages 4 to 16

CHILD'S NAME

PARENT'S TYPE OF WORK (Please be specific—for example: auto mechanic, high school teacher, homemaker, laborer, lathe operator, shoe salesman, army sergeant, even if parent does not live with child.)

SEX	AGE	RACE
☐ Boy		
☐ Girl		

FATHER'S
TYPE OF WORK: _____

MOTHER'S
TYPE OF WORK: _____

TODAY'S DATE | CHILD'S BIRTHDATE

Mo. _____ Day _____ Yr. _____   Mo. _____ Day _____ Yr. _____

THIS FORM FILLED OUT BY:

☐ Mother

☐ Father

☐ Other (Specify):

I. Please list the sports your child most likes to take part in. For example: swimming, baseball, skating, skate boarding, bike riding, fishing, etc.

☐ None

Compared to other children of the same age, about how much time does he/she spend in each?

Compared to other children of the same age, how well does he/she do each one?

	Don't Know	Less Than Average	Average	More Than Average		Don't Know	Below Average	Average	Above Average
a. _____	☐	☐	☐	☐		☐	☐	☐	☐
b. _____	☐	☐	☐	☐		☐	☐	☐	☐
c. _____	☐	☐	☐	☐		☐	☐	☐	☐

II. Please list your child's favorite hobbies, activities, and games, other than sports. For example: stamps, dolls, books, piano, crafts, singing, etc. (Do not include T.V.)

☐ None

Compared to other children of the same age, about how much time does he/she spend in each?

Compared to other children of the same age, how well does he/she do each one?

	Don't Know	Less Than Average	Average	More Than Average		Don't Know	Below Average	Average	Above Average
a. _____	☐	☐	☐	☐		☐	☐	☐	☐
b. _____	☐	☐	☐	☐		☐	☐	☐	☐
c. _____	☐	☐	☐	☐		☐	☐	☐	☐

III. Please list any organizations, clubs, teams, or groups your child belongs to.

☐ None

Compared to other children of the same age, how active is he/she in each?

	Don't Know	Less Active	Average	More Active
a. _____	☐	☐	☐	☐
b. _____	☐	☐	☐	☐
c. _____	☐	☐	☐	☐

IV. Please list any jobs or chores your child has. For example: paper route, babysitting, making bed, etc.

☐ None

Compared to other children of the same age, how well does he/she carry them out?

	Don't Know	Below Average	Average	Above Average
a. _____	☐	☐	☐	☐
b. _____	☐	☐	☐	☐
c. _____	☐	☐	☐	☐

FIGURE 4.7. (*continued*)

V.   1. About how many close friends does your child have?   ☐ None   ☐ 1   ☐ 2 or 3   ☐ 4 or more

     2. About how many times a week does your child do things with them?   ☐ less than 1   ☐ 1 or 2   ☐ 3 or more

VI. Compared to other children of his/her age, how well does your child:

		Worse	About the same	Better
a.	Get along with his/her brothers & sisters?	☐	☐	☐
b.	Get along with other children?	☐	☐	☐
c.	Behave with his/her parents?	☐	☐	☐
d.	Play and work by himself/herself?	☐	☐	☐

VII. 1. Current school performance—for children aged 6 and older:

☐ Does not go to school

	Failing	Below average	Average	Above average
a. Reading or English	☐	☐	☐	☐
b. Writing	☐	☐	☐	☐
c. Arithmetic or Math	☐	☐	☐	☐
d. Spelling	☐	☐	☐	☐
Other academic subjects: for example: history, science, foreign language, geography. e. _____	☐	☐	☐	☐
f. _____	☐	☐	☐	☐
g. _____	☐	☐	☐	☐

2. Is your child in a special class?

☐ No   ☐ Yes—what kind?

3. Has your child ever repeated a grade?

☐ No   ☐ Yes—grade and reason

4. Has your child had any academic or other problems in school?

☐ No   ☐ Yes—please describe

When did these problems start and end?

FIGURE 4.7. (*continued*)

VIII. Below is a list of items that describe children. For each item that describes your child *now* or *within the past 6 months*, please circle the *2* if the item is *very true* or *often true* of your child. Circle the *1* if the item is *somewhat* or *sometimes true* of your child. If the item is *not true* of your child, circle the *0*.

0	1	2	1.	Acts too young for his/her age　16	0	1	2	31.	Fears he/she might think or do something bad
0	1	2	2.	Allergy (describe): _____					
				_____	0	1	2	32.	Feels he/she has to be perfect
					0	1	2	33.	Feels or complains that no one loves him/her
0	1	2	3.	Argues a lot					
0	1	2	4.	Asthma	0	1	2	34.	Feels others are out to get him/her
					0	1	2	35.	Feels worthless or inferior　50
0	1	2	5.	Behaves like opposite sex　20					
0	1	2	6.	Bowel movements outside toilet	0	1	2	36.	Gets hurt a lot, accident-prone
					0	1	2	37.	Gets in many fights
0	1	2	7.	Bragging, boasting					
0	1	2	8.	Can't concentrate, can't pay attention for long	0	1	2	38.	Gets teased a lot
					0	1	2	39.	Hangs around with children who get in trouble
0	1	2	9.	Can't get his/her mind off certain thoughts; obsessions (describe): _____					
					0	1	2	40.	Hears things that aren't there (describe):
0	1	2	10.	Can't sit still, restless, or hyperactive　25					_____　55
					0	1	2	41.	Impulsive or acts without thinking
0	1	2	11.	Clings to adults or too dependent					
0	1	2	12.	Complains of loneliness	0	1	2	42.	Likes to be alone
					0	1	2	43.	Lying or cheating
0	1	2	13.	Confused or seems to be in a fog					
0	1	2	14.	Cries a lot	0	1	2	44.	Bites fingernails
					0	1	2	45.	Nervous, highstrung, or tense　60
0	1	2	15.	Cruel to animals　30					
0	1	2	16.	Cruelty, bullying, or meanness to others	0	1	2	46.	Nervous movements or twitching (describe):
0	1	2	17.	Day-dreams or gets lost in his/her thoughts					_____
0	1	2	18.	Deliberately harms self or attempts suicide	0	1	2	47.	Nightmares
0	1	2	19.	Demands a lot of attention	0	1	2	48.	Not liked by other children
0	1	2	20.	Destroys his/her own things　35	0	1	2	49.	Constipated, doesn't move bowels
0	1	2	21.	Destroys things belonging to his/her family or other children	0	1	2	50.	Too fearful or anxious　65
0	1	2	22.	Disobedient at home	0	1	2	51.	Feels dizzy
0	1	2	23.	Disobedient at school	0	1	2	52.	Feels too guilty
0	1	2	24.	Doesn't eat well	0	1	2	53.	Overeating
0	1	2	25.	Doesn't get along with other children　40	0	1	2	54.	Overtired
0	1	2	26.	Doesn't seem to feel guilty after misbehaving	0	1	2	55.	Overweight　70
0	1	2	27.	Easily jealous	0	1	2	56.	Physical problems without known medical cause:
0	1	2	28.	Eats or drinks things that are not food (describe): _____	0	1	2	a.	Aches or pains
					0	1	2	b.	Headaches
				_____	0	1	2	c.	Nausea, feels sick
					0	1	2	d.	Problems with eyes (describe):
0	1	2	29.	Fears certain animals, situations, or places, other than school (describe): _____	0	1	2	e.	Rashes or other skin problems　75
					0	1	2	f.	Stomachaches or cramps
				_____	0	1	2	g.	Vomiting, throwing up
0	1	2	30.	Fears going to school　45	0	1	2	h.	Other (describe): _____

FIGURE 4.7. *(continued)*

0	1	2	57.	Physically attacks people
0	1	2	58.	Picks nose, skin, or other parts of body (describe): _____

_____ 80

0	1	2	59.	Plays with own sex parts in public 16
0	1	2	60.	Plays with own sex parts too much

0	1	2	61.	Poor school work
0	1	2	62.	Poorly coordinated or clumsy

0	1	2	63.	Prefers playing with older children 20
0	1	2	64.	Prefers playing with younger children

0	1	2	65.	Refuses to talk
0	1	2	66.	Repeats certain acts over and over; compulsions (describe): _____

_____

0	1	2	67.	Runs away from home
0	1	2	68.	Screams a lot 25

0	1	2	69.	Secretive, keeps things to self
0	1	2	70.	Sees things that aren't there (describe):

_____

_____

0	1	2	71.	Self-conscious or easily embarrassed
0	1	2	72.	Sets fires

0	1	2	73.	Sexual problems (describe):

_____

_____ 30

0	1	2	74.	Showing off or clowning

0	1	2	75.	Shy or timid
0	1	2	76.	Sleeps less than most children

0	1	2	77.	Sleeps more than most children during day and/or night (describe): _____

_____

0	1	2	78.	Smears or plays with bowel movements 35

0	1	2	79.	Speech problem (describe): _____

_____

0	1	2	80.	Stares blankly

0	1	2	81.	Steals at home
0	1	2	82.	Steals outside the home

0	1	2	83.	Stores up things he/she doesn't need (describe):

40

0	1	2	84.	Strange behavior (describe): _____

_____

0	1	2	85.	Strange ideas (describe):

_____

0	1	2	86.	Stubborn, sullen, or irritable

0	1	2	87.	Sudden changes in mood or feelings
0	1	2	88.	Sulks a lot 45

0	1	2	89.	Suspicious
0	1	2	90.	Swearing or obscene language

0	1	2	91.	Talks about killing self
0	1	2	92.	Talks or walks in sleep (describe):

_____

0	1	2	93.	Talks too much 50
0	1	2	94.	Teases a lot

0	1	2	95.	Temper tantrums or hot temper
0	1	2	96.	Thinks about sex too much

0	1	2	97.	Threatens people
0	1	2	98.	Thumb-sucking 55

0	1	2	99.	Too concerned with neatness or cleanliness
0	1	2	100.	Trouble sleeping (describe):

_____

0	1	2	101.	Truancy, skips school
0	1	2	102.	Underactive, slow moving, or lacks energy

0	1	2	103.	Unhappy, sad, or depressed 60
0	1	2	104.	Unusually loud

0	1	2	105.	Uses alcohol or drugs (describe):

_____

0	1	2	106.	Vandalism

0	1	2	107.	Wets self during the day
0	1	2	108.	Wets the bed 65

0	1	2	109.	Whining
0	1	2	110.	Wishes to be of opposite sex

0	1	2	111.	Withdrawn, doesn't get involved with others
0	1	2	112.	Worrying

0	1	2	113.	Please write in any problems your child has that were not listed above:

0	1	2		

_____ 70

0	1	2		

_____

0	1	2		

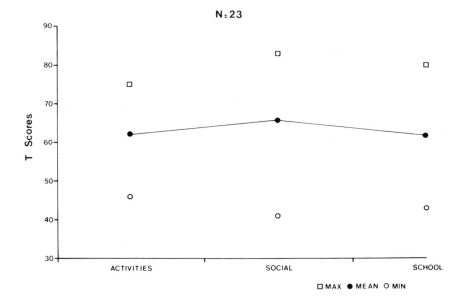

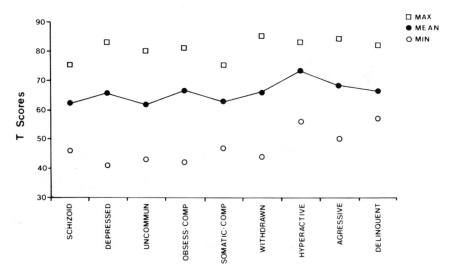

FIGURE 4.8. Child Behavior Checklist (CBCL): Mean, Maximum, and Minimum Scores for Authors' ADD Sample

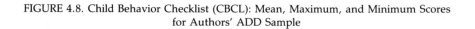

2. How are you getting along at home? (Probe) Any particular problems this week?
3. Do your parents think you need some help? (Probe) Why do they think that? What do they think the problem is?
4. Does your teacher think you need some help? (Probe) Why does he or she think that? What does he or she think the main problem is?
5. What do *you* think? (Probe) Do you have any problems we might be able to help with?

Specific Interview Questions. The questions in Figure 4.9 are restatements of questions asked in the parent interview. Although the child's perception might be quite discrepant from the parent's, it is instructive to determine the child's awareness. The clinician reads the list of questions, and the child chooses one of four cards sized and worded as follows:

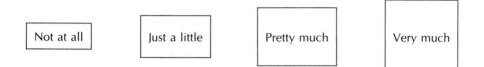

The clinician says: "Some of the children we work with have problems I'd like to tell you about, and then you can tell me to what extent you experience these or similar problems."

Part 2: Attributional Style
Goal. To obtain information and form hypotheses concerning the child's attributional style.

Rationale. ADD children were described in chapter 2 as having particular difficulty on tasks requiring sustained and strategic effort. Although normal children often resist when asked to attend to a task not of their own choosing, among normals the use of incentives or reinforcement usually produces increased effort and better attention.

ADD children, however, respond in atypical and often unpredictable ways to reinforcement contingencies (Douglas, 1984; Kinsbourne, 1984; Wender, 1973). Following praise for working hard, for example, such children might stop working and want to talk to the person who praised them rather than continue working or work harder, as intended. Although the ADD child's atypical responsiveness to reinforcement is generally thought to be related to physiological mechanisms, psychological variables are also involved. Among these psychological vari-

FIGURE 4.9. Child Interview Questions Adapted from DSM III ADD
Diagnostic Criteria

1. Do you often have trouble getting your work finished?
2. Do your mom and your teacher tell you often that you are not listening?
3. Does it bother you to have noise or other people around when you are trying to do your homework?
4. Even if it is quiet do you often have trouble keeping your mind on what you are doing?
5. Is it hard for you to play with just one thing for a long time?
6. Do you do things without thinking carefully first and have other people say, "Why didn't you use your head?"
7. Do you like to play with or work on several things at once and go back and forth from one to the other rather than finishing one thing first?
8. Do you have trouble getting set up and organized? For example, do you have trouble getting all the things you need to be ready for school or to work on an art project before you start out?
9. Do your mom and your teacher have to watch and help you more than the other children?
10. Do you talk or call out in class, forgetting to raise your hand or get permission?
11. Is it hard for you to wait your turn in groups or when playing games?
12. Do you run and climb on things?
13. In your seat at school, is it hard for you to sit still, causing you to squirm around and play with your fingers and things?
14. Do you forget to stay in your seat and have to be reminded to sit down?
15. Do you think you are a toss-and-turn sleeper? For example, are the covers all messed up when you wake up?
16. Do you have more energy than other kids and feel like you can just go and go without stopping?

ables are those related to the child's locus of control. The concept of locus of control (LC) grew from Rotter's (1966) recognition that, when it comes to humans, reinforcements do not stamp in behavior in the manner described by Thorndike. Instead, the effects of reinforcement depend upon an individual's perception of the relationship between his or her behavior and the occurrence of a reinforcing event. Persons who believe that fate, luck, or chance govern their lives (external locus of control) are much less inclined to put forth effort than individuals

FIGURE 4.10. Items from the Nowicki–Strickland Child Locus of Control Scale

1. Do you believe that most problems will solve themselves if you just don't fool with them? YES NO

2. Do you believe that you can stop yourself from catching a cold? YES NO

3. Are some kids just born lucky? YES NO

4. Most of the time do you feel that getting good grades means a great deal to you? YES NO

5. Are you often blamed for things that just are not your fault? YES NO

6. Do you believe that if somebody studies hard enough he or she can pass any subject? YES NO

7. Do you feel that most of the time it doesn't pay to try too hard because things never turn out right anyway? YES NO

8. Do you feel that if things start out well in the morning that it is going to be a good day no matter what you do? YES NO

9. Do you feel that most of the time parents listen to what their children have to say? YES NO

10. Do you believe that wishing can make good things happen? YES NO

11. When you get punished does it usually seem it's for no good reason at all? YES NO

12. Most of the time do you find it hard to change a friend's (mind) opinion? YES NO

13. Do you think that cheering, more than luck, helps a team to win? YES NO

14. Do you feel that it's nearly impossible to change your parent's mind about anything? YES NO

15. Do you believe that your parents should allow you to make most of your own decisions? YES NO

16. Do you feel that when you do something wrong there's very little you can do to make it right? YES NO

17. Do you believe that most kids are just born good at sports? YES NO

18. Are most of the other kids your age stronger than you are? YES NO

FIGURE 4.10. (*continued*)

19. Do you feel that one of the best ways to handle most problems is just not to think about them?
YES   NO

20. Do you feel that you have a lot of choice in deciding who your friends are?
YES   NO

21. If you find a four leaf clover do you believe that it might bring you good luck?
YES   NO

22. Do you often feel that whether you do your homework has much to do with what kind of grades you get?   YES   NO

23. Do you feel that when a kid your age decides to hit you, there's little you can do to stop him or her?
YES   NO

24. Have you ever had a good luck charm?   YES   NO

25. Do you believe that whether or not people like you depends on how you act?   YES   NO

26. Will your parents usually help you if you ask them to?   YES   NO

27. Have you felt that when people were mean to you it was usually for no reason at all?   YES   NO

28. Most of the time, do you feel that you can change what might happen tomorrow by what you do today?   YES   NO

29. Do you believe that when bad things are going to happen they just are going to happen no matter what you try to do to stop them?
YES   NO

30. Do you think that kids can get their own way if they just keep trying?
YES   NO

31. Most of the time do you find it useless to try to get your own way at home?
YES   NO

32. Do you feel that when good things happen they happen because of hard work?   YES   NO

33. Do you feel that when somebody your age wants to be your enemy there's little you can do to change matters?   YES   NO

34. Do you feel that it's easy to get friends to do what you want them to?
YES   NO

35. Do you usually feel that you have little to say about what you get to eat at home?   YES   NO

FIGURE 4.10. (*continued*)

36. Do you feel that when someone doesn't like you there's little you can do about it? YES   NO

37. Do you usually feel that it's almost useless to try in school because most other children are just plain smarter than you are? YES   NO

38. Are you the kind of person who believes that planning ahead makes things turn out better? YES   NO

39. Most of the time, do you feel that you have little to say about what your family decides to do? YES   NO

40. Do you think it's better to be smart than to be lucky? YES   NO

From: "A locus of control scale for children" by S. Nowiki Jr. and B. R. Strickland, 1973, *40*, pp. 148–154. Copyright 1973 by the American Psychological Association. Reproduced by permission.

who see their own efforts (internal locus of control) as the main mechanism for obtaining reinforcements.

General Measure of Locus of Control. Figure 4.10 depicts the items of the Nowiki–Strickland (1973) Child Locus of Control Scale. Responses to these items provide the clinician with a general indication of the extent to which the child is likely, in a wide range of situations and across several types of behavior, to attribute success or failure to external factors or internal factors. For our ADD sample ($N = 23$), the mean external LC score was 15.6, with a minimum score of 4 and a maximum score of 22.

Specific Measures of Attribution in Relation to School Performance and Social Skills. Figure 4.11 depicts interview questions that assess the child's attribution of success and failure in academic and in social situations.

Part III: Awareness of Attentional Variables
Goal. To obtain information regarding the extent to which the child is aware of the general nature of the act of paying attention and the kinds of strategies he might use to increase or focus attention.

Rationale. Patricia Miller and Linda Bigi (1979) developed a structured interview designed to assess children's understanding of the concept of paying attention. Their work built upon earlier work in the area of

FIGURE 4.11. Interview Questions Concerning the Child's
Attributions of Success and Failure in Academic and Social Situations

---

Academic Area

1. "What is your hardest subject in school?" _____
2. "If you get a really bad grade in (name of hardest subject), which of
   the following kinds of things might you be thinking to yourself?"

Place three cards in front of child. Cards a, b, and c state:

Response

_____ Card a—Oh no, I guess I didn't work hard enough on this.

_____ Card b—You know I don't think this teacher likes me very much.

_____ Card c—Ah, what bad luck. I'm having an unlucky day.

Ask the child to close his eyes and vividly picture himself as in a movie
while the grade is being handed back. (Repeat this with good grade in
hardest subject using cards d, e, f.)

Response

_____ Card d—All right, I must have been thinking hard on this.

_____ Card e—Boy, I think the teacher likes me.

_____ Card f—Hey, this is my lucky day.

Social Area

Ask the child to close his eyes and vividly picture himself on the playground at school. A boy whom he has fought with in the past begins to
make fun of his shirt and taunt him. Present cards g, h, and i, and ask the
child: "Which of the following things might you be thinking to yourself?"

Response

Card g—He wants to make me mad but I can handle this. I'll just stay
        cool.

Card h—Other kids don't seem to like me. Why doesn't he just leave me
        alone?

Card i—Boy, is this an unlucky day.

Next ask the child to vividly picture a scene where one of the most
athletic and well liked boys in school is asking him to be on his kickball
team. Present cards j, k, l, and ask the child which statement he might be
thinking to himself.

Card j—Great, he's finally seeing that I'm a good guy and deserve to be
        on his team.

Card k—I'll be darned, he likes me today.

Card l—Hey, I lucked out today. I'll be on the winning team.

metacognition that addressed questions of children's awareness of and ability to regulate thoughts and strategies related to problem solving and memory (Flavell & Wellman, 1977; Kreutzer, Leonard, & Flavell, 1975). The interview questions (depicted in Figures 4.12 and 4.13) that Miller and Bigi developed fall into two parts. During the first part of the interview, the clinician asks the open-ended questions. In using this interview with ADD children, the clinician seeks to learn (a) how aware the children are that they are a sort of information processing system, (b) the degree to which they seem to know that effort is involved in paying attention, and (c) the variables they might suggest as being related to paying attention such as age, motivation, and so on.

The second part of the interview is more structured and seeks to assess the children's awareness of the importance of situational variables such as noise and the presence of others in relation to paying attention. A major area of inquiry concerns children's strategies and their awareness of these strategies for dealing with both internal (e.g., low motivation) and external (e.g., confusing materials) sources of interference.

Miller and Bigi reported a strong developmental trend, with awareness of attention increasing with age. This trend is fairly independent of verbal fluency or expressive abilities concerning the nature and regulation of attention.

Part IV: Child's View of Medication

The fourth and final part of the child interview is administered only to children who are being, or who have recently been, treated with stimulant medication. These interview questions, depicted in Figure 4.14, are intended to obtain input that will increase the clinician's understanding of the child's perception of the intentions and effects of such medication.

Goal. To inquire about the child's own knowledge of and attitudes and feelings toward medication.

Rationale. Particular concerns have been raised about the psychoeducational and psychosocial messages that are given when a child is placed on medication and told that it will increase self-control and self-regulatory abilities.

Whalen and Henker (1980) provided numerous excerpts from child interviews to illustrate the potential negative expectancy a child can develop with regard to his ability to control his own behavior without medication once such medication has been given and its intended effects described. To complicate matters further, the child is often reacted to in different and confusing ways by parents, teachers, siblings, and

FIGURE 4.12. Open-ended Interview Questions from the Miller and
Bigi Interview Concerning What Children Know and Think About
Paying Attention

GENERAL INTERVIEW QUESTIONS

Ability to Pay Attention

Do you know what I mean by "paying attention?" _____
What does it mean? _____
Do you ever have trouble paying attention to something? _____
When? _____
Why do you have trouble paying attention then? _____
When is it easy to pay attention to something? _____
Why? _____
Do you think that younger children and older children are just as good at paying attention? _____
Why? _____

Avoiding Distractions

Pretend you are doing some hard number problems. You are in a room that has a TV, a radio, and a big window through which you can see your friends playing in the park. You want to do a good job on the number problems.

You would have the TV on or off? _____ Why? _____
Would you have the radio on? _____ Why? _____
Would you close the curtain so you couldn't see out the window or would you leave the curtain open so you could see out the window? _____
Why? _____

Responding to a Call

Suppose you are in your room. Your mother comes to the door of your room and calls your name. Her voice is loud enough to reach your ears. Do you think you would always hear her or would there be some times when you don't hear her?

_____

Why? _____
What might you be doing on those times when you don't hear her? ____
Why would you hear her? _____

Attending to Teacher

Suppose your teacher is telling you how to do a new kind of painting with special paints. She is telling you a lot that you have to remember so you have to listen carefully.

How do you listen carefully? _____
Do some children listen more carefully than others? _____
Why? _____
Suppose another person in your class didn't listen carefully. Why might he or she not listen carefully? _____

FIGURE 4.12. (*continued*)

Strategies for Removing Distractions
Imagine you are sitting in the library reading a book. Some children come over near you and talk loudly. Would the noise bother you reading? ___
Why? _____
What could you do so you wouldn't be bothered by the noise? _____

Reproduced by permission of the authors.

FIGURE 4.13. Multiple Choice and Follow-up Type Interview Questions from the Miller and Bigi Interview Concerning What Children Know and Think About Paying Attention

---

SPECIFIC INTERVIEW QUESTIONS

Ability to Pay Attention
Would it be easier to pay attention to something when it's (a) quiet (b) when it's noisy (c) you're interested in it or not (d) you're thinking of other things or not?
Who do you think would be best at paying attention? (a) a 3-year-old (b) an 8-year-old (c) a 15-year-old (d) an adult
Why? _____
Who would be worst? _____ Why? _____
Avoiding Distractions
Pretend you are doing some hard number problems. You are in a room that has a TV, a radio, and a big window through which you can see your friends playing in the park. You want to do a good job on the number problems.
Which would bother your work the most? (a) having the radio on (b) having the TV on (c) leaving the curtain open so you could see your friends playing?
Why? _____
Would _____ (the one not chosen) bother your work? _____
Why? _____
Responding to a Call
Suppose you are in your room. Your mother comes to the door of your room and calls your name. Her voice is loud enough to reach your ears. When are you most likely to hear her? (a) when you're reading an interesting book (b) doing nothing (c) or listening to the radio

---

FIGURE 4.13. (*continued*)

Why? _____

Are you more likely to hear her when you are _____ or _____ (the two not chosen)? Why? _____

Attending to Teacher

Suppose your teacher is telling you how to do a new kind of painting with special paints. She is telling you a lot that you have to remember so you have to listen carefully. Who would listen more carefully to the teacher? (a) a child who is looking at other children (b) talking to other children or not (c) interested in what the teacher is saying or not (d) fooling around or not

Strategies for Removing Distractions

Imagine you are sitting in the library reading a book. Some children come over near you and talk loudly. Would it help your reading if you asked them to (a) be quiet (b) think harder or concentrate (c) put your hands over your ears?

Reproduced by permission of the authors.

peers, who have differing amounts of understanding and expectancies regarding the medicated child.

Following the four-part interview, the child is presented with a number of tasks that allow the clinician to observe and interact with the child in situations and on tasks requiring sustained attention and deliberate problem-solving effort and skills. We begin with a general measure of intelligence, The Wechsler Intelligence Scale for Children (WISC-R) (Weschler, 1974).

WECHSLER INTELLIGENCE SCALE FOR CHILDREN (WISC-R)

The WISC-R is familiar to most clinicians and will not be described in detail here. Sattler (1982) provided detailed information concerning the administration and interpretation of this scale. The subtests of the WISC-R that present the most difficulty for ADD children are coding, arithmetic, and digit span. These three subtests in combination are referred to as *the attention triad*. Although Kaufman (1979) referred to these subtests as measures of freedom from distractibility, they can also be seen as related to attentional capacity and to the ability to focus and sustain attention. Figure 4.15 presents the WISC-R scores and subtest

FIGURE 4.14. Child Interview Questions Concerning the Child's Knowledge, Feelings, and Causal Attributions in Connection with Receiving Stimulant Medication

GENERAL
Your mom says you are (or were) taking some medicine to help you with your problem.
   1. What kind of pills do you take? _____
   2. What are they for? _____
   3. How do they work? _____

SPECIFIC
   1. What would happen if you just stopped taking your pills?
      _____

   2. Pretend a friend tells you he is going to start taking the same medi-
      cine you do, and he wants to know what it will do. What would
      you tell him?
      _____
      _____

   3. Can other people tell if you don't take your medicine? _____
      _____

   4. Do you think you could fool your mom or your teacher into thinking
      you have taken your pills when you really haven't _____ (If Yes)
      How would you do that? (If No) Why would that be so hard?
      _____

   5. Do you think if we both work real hard on your problems we could
      teach you to do ok without your pills? _____
      _____

Questions adapted from Henker and Whalen, 1980; Whalen and Henker, 1976.

scores for our ADD sample. Note that, for our sample, the attention triad subtests are the lowest of the WISC-R subtests.

ACHIEVEMENT TESTS

Achievement test scores, like intelligence test scores, would not be expected to reflect improvement as the result of a short-term interven-tion program, and achievement measures are seldom included in out-come studies. Yet, because achievement tests are an important long-

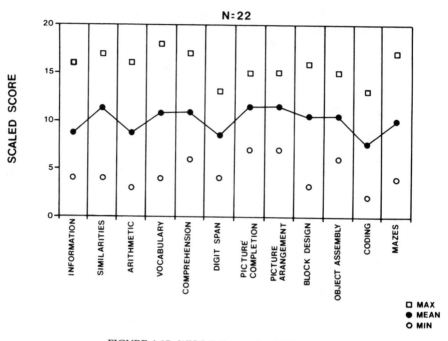

FIGURE 4.15. WISC-R Scores for ADD Sample

term goal of intervention, it seems quite worthwhile to include at least one such measure in the assessment battery. The Wide Range Achievement Test (WRAT) (Jastak & Jastak, 1978) provides a quick measure of three different ability areas: reading (actually word recognition), spelling, and arithmetic. The Peabody Individual Achievement Test (PIAT) (Dunn & Markwardt, 1970) takes a bit longer to administer (30–40 minutes) but assesses reading comprehension and general information in addition to reading, spelling, and arithmetic.

Although both the WRAT and the PIAT provide useful information concerning the achievement level of ADD children, they do not provide a good basis for a task analysis directed toward finding the specific reasons for a child's poor performance in the separate subject areas. Specialized tests such as the Gray Oral Reading Test or the Durrell measure of reading comprehension provide more detailed and useful information for the clinician who wants to do a task analysis and focus treatment on specific problem areas.

Figure 4.16 depicts the PIAT profile for a sample of 22 ADD children.

N=22

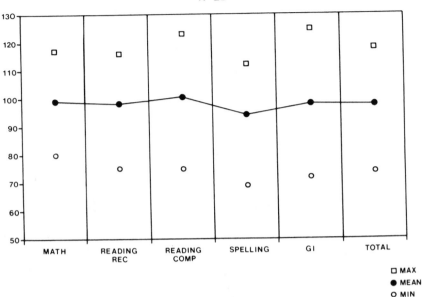

□ MAX
● MEAN
○ MIN

FIGURE 4.16. PIAT Standard Scores for ADD Samples

MATCHING FAMILIAR FIGURES
TEST (MFF)

Developmental psychology has, in the last 20 years, focused much attention on a dimension called *conceptual tempo* (Kagan, 1966). The extremes of this dimension are known as *reflectivity* on the one end and *impulsivity* on the other. In research and in treatment programs for ADD, the MFF is the major, and often the only, measure of impulsivity–reflectivity used. The MFF is a match-to-sample type test in which the subject attempts to locate among six competing alternatives the picture or drawing that most closely resembles the standard at the top of the page (see Figure 4.17). The choices are similar enough that the task requires a careful search and comparison of the various possibilities. The examiner records both the latency to first response and the total number of errors. Impulsivity–reflectivity is operationally defined as the composite of latency and errors.

There has been a good deal of discussion in the literature regarding the reliability of the MFF, the adequacy of the norms, the best way of combining latency and error scores, and so on. Whatever the outcome of these debates and discussions, the test continues to be widely used;

FIGURE 4.17. Sample Item from the Matching Familiar Figures Test (MFF)

and, in our experience, the MFF has considerable clinical utility with ADD children, especially when it is administered in an *interactive* way. This means that once the test has been administered according to the standard directions, the clinician goes back to the first item, saying, for example:

> *Clinician:* Some of those were pretty hard, but you really worked on them. Some kids really can't find the right answers at all. What I would like for you to do now is to go back and tell me what your main plan, or strategy, for finding correct answers was.
> *Chad:* I don't know. I just look them over till I see the right one.
> *Clinician:* But what if the one you said was correct was really not quite

right, like on the ones where I said, "That's not quite right," and I
asked you to try again.

Chad: Well, I just tried again.

Clinician: What if you were wrong again?

Chad: Same thing.

Clinician: But then you've made two mistakes or errors. What if it were
extremely important for you to make as few errors as possible? What
might you do, for example, if I gave you a hundred dollars and took
ten dollars every time you made a mistake?

Chad: Man, for a hundred dollars I wouldn't make no mistakes.

Clinician: But what plan or strategy would you use?

Chad: (Without hesitation) I'd go real slow and make sure it was the right
one, before I guessed.

Clinician: Yeah, and how would you *know* you were right?

Chad: Cause I'd think before I guessed.

Clinician: Think. Yes, I like that better than guess. Tell me Chad, what
exactly do you *think* when you are trying to find the right one? Let's
go back over some of these, and you tell me exactly what your thoughts
were, OK?

The clinician proceeds in this manner, trying to tease out the strategy
or lack of strategic thinking involved. If a child seems reluctant or unable to describe his thoughts or strategy, the clinician might tell him to
pretend that he is teaching a younger child how to do well on this test.
We have also had the child being assessed actually teach another child
his strategy on tasks such as the MFF while we listened in. This type
of inquiry yields a valuable sample of the nature of attentional and
information processing problems.

Neil J. Salkind at the University of Kansas has developed norms for
the MFF that help the clinician interpret the results of an individual
child's performance.* Cairns and Cammock (1978) developed a longer
and more reliable version of the MFF called the MFF-20, and they have
collected norms for this extended version. The MFF-20 is the version
we now use. A preschool version of the MFF has also been developed
by Wright (1973).

The mean latency score for our ADD sample ($N = 22$) on the MFF-20
was 14.8 seconds, with a minimum of 4.6 seconds and a maximum of
53 seconds. For error scores, the mean was 20.7 seconds, with a minimum of 2 seconds and a maximum of 43 seconds. The younger children in our sample made more errors and had shorter latency scores,
but the variability was still considerable.

The reader who is interested in using the MFF as a research tool or
who intends to make extensive reference to latency scores or combined
latency and error scores should consult two extensive and thoughtful

---

*Personal correspondence.

papers by Victor, Halverson, and Montague (1985), and Gjerde, Block, and Block (1985).

CHILDREN'S EMBEDDED FIGURES TEST (CEFT)

The CEFT was developed by Karp and Konstadt (1971). Tasks such as the CEFT require the client to locate a particular geometric shape such as a tent or a house from among a confusing array of lines and shapes. The disembedding of the selected stimulus figure requires the child to put effort into searching the figures in a careful and organized manner. The child must also inhibit the tendency to respond to shapes that resemble the target stimulus but are incorrect.

In that the CEFT pulls for sustained focused attention, it provides the clinician with an excellent measure of, and opportunity to observe the processes involved in, the act of paying attention. As with the MFF, asking the child to verbalize his strategies and frustrations while trying to disembed the figures has potential for enriching the amount and quality of information obtained from the CEFT. The sample mean of 22 ADD children in our program was 13.4, with a minimum score of 2 and a maximum score of 22.

ASSESSMENT OF AROUSAL LEVELS

The view that defective control of arousal level is one of the primary factors associated with ADD is widely shared. Despite the controversy that has surrounded the issue of stimulant medication as an aid to arousal control, such medication has a clear role to play in the treatment of ADD children. Whether or not a child is currently taking medication, the clinician needs to be aware of the control or lack of control the child has over his own level of arousal.

In our work we have experimented with physiological measures such as the galvanic skin response and electromyographic recordings. These have not proven particularly useful. Following the example of Virginia Douglas, we have attempted to include the control of arousal in both our assessment and treatment sequences with ADD children. Douglas (1980), in emphasizing the importance of arousal levels, stated:

> We have only recently begun to appreciate the possible importance of helping hyperactive children gain better control over their own arousal or alertness. Consequently when we carried out our two training studies (Douglas, Parry, Marton, & Garson 1976; and Garson 1977) we did not

emphasize teaching techniques for accomplishing this in a consistent fashion. . . . In the meantime, however, we have begun to draw the children's attention to their own arousal states during the sessions; we try, also, to make them aware that certain tasks make particular demands for alertness and commitment on their part. Occasionally, these children arrive at a session in a state that appears "high" and erratic so that serious work is impossible. Since experience has shown that the same behaviors may not be repeated in the following sessions, we try to engage in activities that will avoid confrontations and, hopefully, help the children become more controlled. (p. 310)

Along these same lines, parents often comment about behavior when they drop a child off for treatment, saying "Good luck today" or "Boy, is he wound up today," or "He seems calmer today." Noticing that parents seem to be aware of fluctuations of their child's arousal, we began asking for a parent rating of child arousal at the beginning of each treatment session. They rate on a simple 5 point scale.

1	2	3	4	5
very calm	fairly calm	average /calm	somewhat wound up	very wound up

These ratings have proven helpful in a number of ways, not all of which we planned or anticipated. One, they help our clinicians decide how to begin the session. If a parent rates a child as being at level 4 or 5, we begin with a calming or relaxation procedure. Such procedures range from simply having the child take several deep breaths, repeating softly and slowly words like *calm, smooth, slow, easy,* and *relax,* to more extensive Jacobson-type exercises (1938) in which the clinician has the child lie on a mat while the clinician or a tape-recorded voice takes him through relaxation of the various muscle groups, beginning at the top of the head and proceeding down the body to the toes.

A second use of arousal ratings is to determine what, if any, immediate effects the treatment is having on the child's ability to control his own arousal level. The ratings are charted on a simple line graph showing the fluctuations and possible trends of these fluctuations. Parents can sometimes provide insights into situational variables that relate to fluctuations in their child's arousal level. One mother, for example, looked at the graph and said, "You know what, several of those high points are on days after he was with his father." This child's parents had recently been separated, and the child alternated 3 or 4 days with each.

A third use of arousal ratings, and one that was not anticipated, occurred when Charlette, an 11-year-old girl, overheard her mother discussing the rating of 5 for her daughter's arousal level. Charlette, who was unusually wound up that day, forcefully argued that she was a 3, not a 5, and eventually compromised at 4. After this incident, we began having Charlette rate her own level of arousal at the beginning and at the end of each session. In addition, the clinician also began rating Charlette as a sort of judge or third-party arbitrator when Charlette and the mother disagreed. These ratings stimulated extended discussion regarding the cues or signs that Charlette used in determining her own ratings, as well as an appreciation of the more outwardly noticeable cues that were used by the mother and by the clinician. All three ratings were used to help monitor and evaluate the effect of treatment.

We now use similar 5-point rating and self-rating scales to evaluate such things as the kind of day a child had at school, general attentiveness during sessions and selected school periods, the degree of cooperation or fairness exhibited during games or play situations (both in and out of treatment), and the extent to which a child remembered and used various skills taught during treatment in real-life situations, such as resistance to anger provocation. These ratings have been particularly useful in the social skills area.

SOCIAL COGNITION MEASURES

During the past few years an increasing number of instruments purporting to measure social cognition and interpersonal problem-solving skills have been developed. Problems in establishing adequate reliability and validity that plagued earlier and more traditional personality measures are apparent too among these new measures. Yet, when these new measures are used with appropriate caution and viewed as sources for hypotheses and not conclusions concerning the maladaptive social responses of ADD children, several appear promising. Chapter 6 describes the social adjustment problems of ADD children and the assessment measures that relate to such problems.

SUMMARY

Assessment of ADD children being considered for cognitive training takes into account the available knowledge concerning the nature and etiology of the disorder and is also based on the unique requirement of this treatment approach. As such, it has taken several years to settle on our current battery of evaluation procedures. As with our whole attitude toward ADD children, we maintain a spirit of investigative playfulness. We do and will evolve, as we did with Charlette's improvisation. But we are confident we have a solid basis of screening criteria and evaluative measurement.

Parent and child interviews are conducted in order to obtain both objective information and parent and child perceptions of the problem. Parents and children are involved as extensively as possible in describing the major targets for treatment and in formulating an agreed-upon treatment plan. As treatment progresses, parents and children are also involved as much as possible in monitoring treatment effects and in making decisions regarding changes in target selection or in procedures.

The more traditional tools of assessment, intelligence and achievement tests, are employed in an interactive manner with the goal of observing the child in the process of attending and problem solving rather than for the sole purpose of obtaining the products (standard scores). Tests such as the MFF and the CEFT allow the clinician to observe the child's learning and problem-solving style and difficulties. Finally, the child, the parent, and the clinician supplement the assessment picture through periodic ratings of such variables as arousal level, quality of attention, and overall adjustment and progress in the home, school, and clinic.

Chapter 5

Basic Components of Cognitive–Behavioral Training

We have described the attention deficit disorder child as having two major kinds of problems that have visible behavioral referents. These problems are (a) inability to focus and sustain attention during problem solving and (b) poor inhibition of responding (impulsivity) in both academic and social problem-solving situations. Two other less visible characteristics that often accompany and can be causally related to inattention and impulsivity are poorly modulated arousal levels and apparent lack of normal responsiveness to rewards or reinforcements. In our efforts to understand the mechanisms that govern attention, arousal, and impulse control, we have become convinced, for reasons outlined in earlier chapters, that language, or inner speech, plays an important and, indeed, a crucial role. This chapter describes the basic components and procedures used in Cognitive–Behavioral Training to increase ADD childrens' use of language or inner speech as a means of reducing impulsivity and increasing attentiveness. The three procedures described are Verbal Self-Instruction, Response–Cost, and Cognitive Monitoring. Social Skills Training, a fourth major component of our program, is described in chapter 6.

VERBAL SELF-INSTRUCTION TRAINING (VSI)

Previous chapters described the ADD child as having problems devising and using deliberate cognitive strategies to meet the demands of academic and social problem-solving situations. *Attention deficit* was broadly defined as involving the failure of cognitive events, processes, and structures to mediate and regulate behavior. The Soviet psychologists Vygotsky (1962) and Luria (1959, 1982) prepared a model to explain how normal children acquire these cognitive mediating processes. The Vygotsky and Luria model has been translated into a self-instructional training program that involves modeling the use of inner speech or self-instructions for the child. Modeling by the clinician is followed by a set of carefully prescribed steps for teaching the child to use verbal self-instructions in his own problem-solving attempts. The effectiveness of this type of training has been evaluated by a number of investigators, with encouraging results (Douglas, Parry, Marton, & Garson, 1976; Hinshaw, Henker, & Whalen, 1984; Konstantareas & Hermatidis, 1983; Meichenbaum & Goodman, 1971; Palkes, Stewart, & Freedman, 1972; Palkes, Stewart, & Kahana, 1968).

Verbal Self-Instruction Training involves a number of steps, which will be explained with examples when necessary. The steps to be described are

1. Task Selection
2. Cognitive Modeling (six stages)
3. Overt External Guidance
4. Overt Self-Guidance
5. Modeling of Faded Overt Self-Guidance
6. Child Practice of Faded Overt Self-Guidance
7. Modeling of Covert Self-Instruction
8. Child Practice of Covert Self-Instruction

Step One: Task Selection

The clinician selects tasks that involve sustained focused attention and require the use of some type of systematic plan or strategy for successful completion. Information gained from the assessment procedures should be used to help the clinician select tasks with an appropriate level of difficulty for the child.

Example:
For the child who has performed poorly on the Matching Familiar Figures Test, the clinician could select a similar match-to-sample task.

Step Two: Cognitive Modeling

The clinician models the solution of the task. This modeling involves the clinician's talking himself or herself through the following six problem-solving stages:

Defining and Understanding the Nature of the Task
Example:
Clinician: "Let's see, I'm supposed to find the cowboy that looks just like the one below. The problem here is that all six cowboys up here look just alike. I could just pick any of them, but that would be guessing. I need some way to be sure I get the right one."

Generating Possible Ways of Approaching the Task
Example:
Clinician: "I could look carefully at each cowboy and then choose, but they might all still look the same. Maybe I could pick two or three that look the closest alike and then compare them with each other. Or maybe I could eliminate them one at a time until there is only one left.

Selecting a Strategy and Applying it
Example:
Clinician: "If I really want to do well at this, I'd better take my time and look at each one closely. I guess I'll try the elimination plan. OK, cowboy number one. Hat's the same, shirt's the same, buckle's the same—whoops! No, it isn't. Cross out cowboy number one. Cowboy two. Ah, the hat's smaller. I bet it's number three. Yeah, he looks good. I pick this one. But wait, my plan was to look at *each* one. Better keep going. Number three is a maybe. Now number four is out; his gun is missing. Number five. H'mmm, he looks the same as three. Number six is way out, his boots don't have heels. So, is it three or is it five? Let me compare each of them. Ah, I see it. Three has no buttons on his shirt. It's number five, and I'm sure of it. On to the next problem."

Self-Monitoring of Progress Toward Solution
Example:
At periodic intervals the clinician asks herself or himself, "How is this working out? My strategy was to use the elimination method, and it seems to work. I have to be careful not to start guessing though. This is hard work and kind of boring, but I've got to stick it out. Only three more problems."

Self Evaluation and Self-Reward
Example:
Clinician: "Done. Finally. Not bad; I think I got them all right. Except maybe the spaceship one. That was hard. I think I'll go back and check that one again. Let's see, it was four or six, and I picked six. Oh, Oh, the nose cone is too pointed. Let's look at four. That's it. Now I think I have them all right. Good for me. I usually do terribly on any problem that you have to be careful on, but if I settle down and talk myself through with a plan that I stick with, I can do as well as anybody. Maybe better. What a thinker I am. Class act."

Selecting an Alternative Approach when Unsuccessful
> *Example:*
> Clinician: "I'm working hard on this, but I keep making mistakes. I'd better check my strategy. I think I need a whole new approach here."

Step Three: Overt External Guidance

Next, the clinician has the child complete the task while the clinician verbally instructs him through it, following the same six problem-solving stages

> *Example:*
> The clinician says, "Now you solve the next one and I'll do your thinking for you. OK, you're looking at all the possible answers and thinking . . . what am I doing here now? I'm trying to find one that's exactly like the one below. What plan could I follow? I could pick this one, but wait, my plan was to look at *each* one carefully and eliminate them one at a time. Here I go."

Step Four: Overt Self-Guidance

Then, the clinician has the child complete the task again (or a similar one) while using the child's own self-statements to guide him toward a solution. This is a difficult step to teach because it requires the child's active involvement. Instead of considering steps three and four as separate procedures, the clinician should go back and forth (between this one and overt external guidance) by prompting the child's thoughts and then letting the child finish the thought.

> *Example:*
> Clinician: "Well, number three is eliminated, now I will. . . ."
> Child: "Check number four."
> Clinician: "Let's see, the hat is. . . ."
> Child: "The same. The shirt is the same. The gun is—oh, oh, it's different."

During this step the clinician begins to capture the nature of the child's natural way of self-instructing and notes the kinds of self-statements used by the child. The clinician also notes the types of self-statements that would appear to help but are not being generated by the child. For example, the child might habitually avoid statements directing himself to consider the nature of a problem carefully and to pause to choose a deliberate strategy before beginning work on a task. He could also lack coping statements to deal with the frustration of being stuck. Modeling samples of each of these types of self-statements follow.

Task definition statements, for example, for a match-to-sample task such as the MFF, a clinician could model like this: "What kind of problem is this? I need to figure out which one up here exactly matches the one below."

Coping self-statements to be modeled might include

"Wow, this is driving me nuts. I need to slow myself down and start over. I'll just go slow and easy. Boy this is hard. I can't do it. I'll just have to give up. Oh, no, I'm not supposed to say that. Now what do I do when I'm stuck? Oh yeah, let me see if there is another way of looking at this."

Step Five: Modeling of Faded Overt Self-Guidance

The clinician models the whispering of the instructions to himself or herself while going through the task.

We have found that children are sometimes even more self-conscious about whispering than they are about talking to themselves. Rather than insisting that they actually whisper, we model and teach self-instructing in a low, barely audible tone. This step in the VSI training also demonstrates the disjointed, fragmented type of instructions that are more characteristic of the inner speech or thoughts we are attempting to develop. For example, a clinician might need to model

"Check two. Nope. Three. Hat. Buckle. Ah, ha, nope. Number four. Whew—boring. Stick it out. Careful. I think it's number five. Check six again. Yeah, it's five. Good. Not many more. Hang in there, hang in."

Step Six: Child Practice of Faded Overt Self-Guidance

The objective here is to help the child see the nature and usefulness of genuine self-instructions. The clinician listens carefully to the child and helps him generate his own thoughts and self-instructions rather than allowing him to copy the clinician.

Step Seven: Modeling of Covert Self-Instruction

In modeling this stage, the clinician moves his or her lips, looks pensive, pauses to check two alternatives by pointing at one and then the other, and so on. Also, the child is told before the task is modeled the kinds of things the clinician will be thinking about.

Step Eight: Child Practice of Covert Self-Instruction

This is the final step in Verbal Self-Instruction Training. The child now has to think his own way through the task at hand. Because this involves covert self-instruction, the clinician is unable to monitor directly the child's thinking. But observation of the child's behavior (e.g., did he evaluate two alternatives by pointing to one and then the other?) provides some clues to the clinician about how the child is approaching the task. To check how the child is providing self-instruction, the clinician might need to ask some clarifying questions such as

"What were you thinking just now?"
"Tell me the strategy you just used."

INVOLVING THE ADD CHILD IN VSI TRAINING

Equipped with the outline of a plausible theory and the previous description of VSI training, a well-intentioned clinician could readily teach children to use VSI, it would appear. But our experience, and the experience of others (Bash & Camp, 1980), indicates that such is often not the case. Considering the chronic and pervasive nature of the problems of ADD children, it should not be surprising that they do not enter easily into a treatment requiring their genuine and intensive involvement. How, then, does one get ADD children who are either passively inattentive and daydreamy or slapdash, overresponsive, and unmotivated to cooperate sufficiently for the application of treatment procedures? Meichenbaum (1977) has provided some recommendations that are helpful for dealing with this problem. Among his suggestions are the following

1. The therapist should be animated and responsive to the child.
2. Treatment should begin with games or activities that relate to the child's own medium of play.
3. The child should not be allowed to self-instruct in a mechanical or rote manner.

We incorporated these suggestions in our treatment program, with positive results. But this took considerable refinement time. We found that clinicians could not employ these recommendations automatically without practice and critical feedback. These suggestions therefore need further elaboration.

Be Animated and Responsive with the Child

Daily review of videotaped sessions revealed that the clinicians related to the children in a kind and sincere, but often unanimated, manner. In response, the children often adopted a role of compliance but failed to invest genuine effort in tasks. It is difficult for many clinicians to be truly animated with a child in CBM training. Persons who relate within professional roles, such as psychologists, teachers, or physicians, often adopt the mannerisms associated with such roles. Children, however, are highly sensitive to the difference between formal encounters with a role and genuine encounters with a person. Authenticity on the part of the clinician best elicits genuine response and effort from ADD children involved in treatment.

Begin Treatment with Interesting Games, Not Academic Tasks

The use of games or art activities is often suggested as a means of establishing rapport with children who are being evaluated or treated. The use of such activities in conjunction with cognitive training, however, has a very different purpose. Games are most apt for ADD children, because most of these children, by the time they enter treatment, have a history of failure with academic tasks such as decoding words, spelling, and arithmetic. We recently asked a fourth-grade boy in our clinic to read a passage from his social studies book. When he stopped at a word he apparently could not recognize, we asked him about his strategy for figuring out unfamiliar words. He looked quizzically and said, "Nothing. If you don't know, you have to ask somebody." When we attempted to show him how to sound out the word, he groaned, "I've tried all that stuff. It don't work for me. I have a reading disability." Rather than attempting to convince this boy that his reading disability was another name for a lack of strategies for decoding unfamiliar words, we began by trying to hook him on the general notion of developing strategies through the use of games.

Selecting games and interesting tasks when success is still desired and when cognitive strategies are required offers the clinician a fresh chance to model and teach strategic thinking before moving on to areas in which the child has already fought and lost many battles. From a retrospective look at our own past efforts, it seems likely that the initial use of games has often been too quickly abandoned in our eagerness to get to the "real problems" described in the referrals. Anxious concern about a child's academic and social skills on the part of the parents can lead to early skepticism and criticism about treatment when the child informs them that, "Today, we just played Uno" (a simple card game requiring some strategy). Unless parents are fully informed about and involved in the treatment program, they can, and often do, pressure the clinician to move on to "more important things," make discouraging remarks about the treatment in front of their child, or even withdraw the child from treatment.

Discourage Rote, Uninvolved Self-Instructing

It is extremely important that treatment subjects do not self-instruct in a rote and monotonous manner. If we truly expect these children to gradually incorporate self-instructions into a habitual and useful self-dialogue, the tone of their self-statements must ring true. As clinicians, we need to ask the question, "If this child were to think about this problem in a more reflective manner, what words would he be likely to use?"

In this vein, Vygotsky (1962) noted that, when speech becomes internalized, it is not really like faded speech. It is instead abbreviated and ungrammatical. The ability of the clinician to capture the tone of natural abbreviated thought should increase the naturalness of the child's self-instructions. If the child persists in employing a monotonous tone, the clinician should alternate modeling an animated, convincing self-dialogue with the less convincing tone the child is using. For example, while solving a word-hunt problem the clinician would say in a monotonous tone

> "What is my problem? My problem is to find and circle the words on this list. What strategy shall I use? (dully) I will go slow and look carefully."

The clinician then begins to look at the matrix of scrambled letters, repeating the first word on the list.

> "Airway, Airway, where is the word Airway? Wait a minute, I'm not really using a strategy, I'm just saying words." With a more energetic and involved voice, the clinician might continue, "What *is* the problem here? The problem is that these words are hidden among the rows and columns of letters. I'm just looking at the letters and waiting for the word to jump out at me, and it doesn't work. Some of the words are backwards and some are written on the diagonal backwards. Those are really hard to see. I know. I'll start at the top and go along each row looking for the first letter *A*. When I find an *A*, I will look at each letter next to it for the *i*. If I find it, I will look for the *r* and so on. *Now* (eagerly) I have a real strategy. If I stick with it, I can't miss."

Teaching ADD children to engage in meaningful self-instructing behaviors is a demanding task. The transition from a slapdash "guess-and-go" style to a careful reflective style is not easily accomplished. Frequently there is resistance from the child. An effective tool for overcoming initial resistance is response–cost.

RESPONSE–COST

Meichenbaum (1977) has suggested that VSI Training should be supplemented with an operant procedure such as response–cost. The effectiveness of the response–cost procedure as a behavior-change technique has been well documented (Kendall & Finch, 1976, 1978). In its simplest form, response–cost involves providing the child with a number of tokens at the beginning of each treatment session. The child is told that, if he abides by the rules of the session—for example, by not looking up while working, staying in his seat, and not talking—he will not lose any tokens. If he violates one of these rules, however, a token is removed. At the end of each session, the child can spend his remaining tokens for small prizes or save his tokens for larger prizes later on. These prizes should be selected by the child from a reward menu that he can help to prepare.

Used in this simple fashion, response–cost functions as a behavioral-control device. Our experience with this procedure is that rather striking changes result almost immediately after it is introduced. In small groups of four or five children, the effects are even more pronounced than when it is applied in a one-on-one session. If the goal of treatment were to create an orderly learning environment in which impulsive and inattentive children merely appear to be reflective and attentive, response–cost alone would accomplish much of this objective. Our goal, however, is to produce self-control rather than environmental control, and this requires an adaptation of the response–cost procedure.

Not surprisingly, when the response–cost procedure is introduced to our student clinicians, the reaction is often negative. The type of question we have come to expect is, "How can I develop the type of sensitive rapport necessary for true modeling in the VSI training, when I am essentially punishing the child at frequent intervals?" The answer to this question lies in part in the way in which response–cost is introduced and employed.

When response–cost is introduced, young children especially could react strongly to the "Indian giver" notion of having something given to them and then taken away. Anticipating this attitude, we begin by saying that the tokens are there to be earned by the child for his efforts in acquiring some important new skills that will help him at home and at school. He is told, at the onset, that he will almost certainly lose quite a few tokens during the early sessions, while these skills are being learned. Used as a behavior-modification tool, the removal of tokens would be viewed as a punishment procedure. In cognitive training, however, the tokens are used more as feedback than as punishment. This is made as clear as possible to the child and clarified by low-keyed feedback from the clinician as response–cost is employed.

Using information from the assessment folder, the clinician discusses the behaviors or targets the child needs to work on. The clinician explains that the first step in changing one's behavior is to become aware of the occurrence of problem behaviors. Removing tokens is a clear message that problem behavior is occurring. Padawer, Zupan, and Kendall (1980) have described in some detail the use of two types of feedback to be provided when tokens are removed. The first type is concrete information in which the clinician simply identifies and labels the behavior. For example, "Charles, you talked out of turn" or "Pat, you stopped working and started fiddling with your shoe." This is said in a calm, matter-of-fact manner with frequent reassurance that learning to change behaviors that have become habitual takes time and practice.

The second type of feedback is conceptual feedback. With this, the clinician tries to clarify for the child the meaning of the behaviors that resulted in his referral. For example, instead of saying, "Ralph, I am taking away a token, because you blurted out the answer," the clinician would say, "Ralph, you are being impulsive again." Or instead of saying, "You were staring out into space," the clinician would say, "You are being inattentive." During the course of treatment, the clinician reduces the use of concrete labeling of behaviors and shifts toward conceptual feedback. This is done because research has shown that, although concrete feedback provides clear and unambiguous information to the child, the use of conceptual labeling promotes transfer of learning to real-life situations.

After progressing from concrete to conceptual feedback, we can later shift away from targeting behavior problems that caused the referral, such as being inattentive and impulsive, and begin to target more positive behaviors related to involvement in treatment such as the use of clear, meaningful, or involved-sounding self-statements or the actual performance of self-instructions. The clinician might say, "Peter, I'm going to take a token here to remind you to say that you are really thinking as you solve this problem. If you think it's too hard or boring or you're just plain stuck, then say it out loud. Then I can help you deal with getting unstuck."

In summary, the response–cost procedure can be a very effective means of getting the child to settle down during the initial phase of treatment and can later be an effective tool for obtaining fuller involvement in VSI training. Again, the clinician should keep in mind the long-term goal of treatment, which is to increase self-control rather than to allow or encourage others to exert more control over the child. As such, some thought should be given to phasing out the use of tangible rewards by shifting to more natural ones such as playing a game after the session, sharing a coke, or just providing time to talk about whatever the child chooses. A later chapter discusses the shifting of treatment away from the clinic setting toward the home and school, where many natural rewards are available.

COGNITIVE MONITORING

Cognitive monitoring is a procedure that can be used either by itself or in conjunction with the other procedures we have just described. As we indicate later, it is a procedure that is particularly effective with some ADD children, but, for others it is a procedure that is best delayed until later in treatment. The basic cognitive monitoring procedure has been described and well researched by Kneedler and Hallahan (1981). With this procedure, the child is taught to respond to a tape recording of a bell that sounds at irregular intervals by indicating whether or not he was paying attention each time the bell sounded. After training, the child is given practice in the use of this procedure. His desk is affixed with a strip of paper that is demarcated with columns marked yes and no, and seatwork tasks are assigned. The child works at an assigned task until the bell sounds and then puts a check mark in the "yes" column if he thinks he was paying attention when it sounded and in the "no" column if he is aware of his inattentiveness. As the child's awareness of his attentiveness, or lack of it, increases, the interval is lengthened, requiring longer periods of sustained attention without an external reminder.

Reflective children, who do not have an attention deficit disorder, are capable of making self-statements such as, "I'd better complete this paper in the 25 minutes left, or else I'll have to stay in for recess." The ADD child is cued by the bell to have a modicum of such self-reflective thought.

It is interesting to note that Kneedler and his colleagues have found that the accuracy of the child's self-reports immediately after the bell rings is not significantly related to either improvement in attending behaviors or achievement, with improvements occurring in both attention and achievement regardless of the accuracy of self-reports. That is, even if the child's reports that he was paying attention when the bell sounded are frequently not in agreement with those of a person who observed him, that child still continues to improve in attending as use of the bell continues.

In the application of self-monitoring with our clinic population, we have noted that children, who already possess skills for attending to and solving a particular task, but who consistently fail to use them, benefit readily from the self-monitoring procedure. Such children have been described in the literature as having a production deficiency (Flavell, Beach, & Chinsky, 1966). Children who have true mediation deficiencies in the form of skill and strategy deficits, however, might simply learn to appear more attentive without accompanying gains in actual problem-solving skills. When such children are identified, it is best to delay the introduction of cognitive monitoring until later in treatment.

We have also recently begun to explore the application of self-monitoring as an extension of VSI training rather than applying it to the broader class of inattentive behaviors. Here we provide the child with a checklist containing rows that list the six problem-solving stages taught during VSI training: (a) defining and understanding the problem, (b) generating a number of possible strategies for solving the problem, (c) choosing and applying a deliberate strategy, (d) sticking with this strategy and monitoring progress, (e) congratulating oneself if the strategy is successful, and (f) going back and selecting an alternative approach if it is not. When the bell sounds, the child checks the column that best describes the nature of the cognitive activity he was engaging in immediately preceding the sound of the bell. Here again, it is not so important that the child accurately identify the specific thoughts; rather, the function of the bell is to constantly remind the child that systematic thinking is required in order to do well on the task.

SOCIAL SKILLS TRAINING

Children who have difficulties in the self-regulation of behavior during academic problem solving also are frequently unable to adjust to the complex demands of situations requiring social and interpersonal skills. Our early summer programs did not include direct training in the social skills area; rather we assumed and hoped that, by being taught to become more strategic and deliberate in solving academic problems, the children would then apply or transfer these skills into the social arena. When it became clear that this was not occurring, we began planning for such transfer to occur. Chapter 6 describes in detail the manner in which we teach social and interpersonal skills to ADD children.

SUMMARY

This chapter has described the basic components and procedures used in a cognitive–behavioral approach for the ADD child. An effort was made to describe these procedures in sufficient detail to enable the clinician to begin to conduct such cognitive training. Rather than being a static method of treatment, the cognitive–behavioral approach lends itself to flexible adaptations that correspond with the individual characteristics of each ADD child. The following chapter describes ways in which these procedures have been combined and supplemented with further ideas from the general literature and research concerning problem solving.

Chapter 6

Interpersonal Problem-Solving and Social Skills Training

Interpersonal problems and social skill deficits are not listed in the DSM III as major problem areas for ADD children. However, in that interpersonal and social difficulties are as omnipresent among such children as inattention, impulsivity, and hyperactivity, and because social skill deficits are a most common initiating referral cause, a strong case could be made for their inclusion as a core symptom area. Though parents and teachers are frustrated and perplexed by the social ineptness of ADD children, they often stress the point that a particular child being referred is not a "bad" child. They cite incidents in which a child's exuberance resulted in an unanticipated and unfortunate result. This careless exuberance is just one of a number of common social tendencies of preschool and kindergarten children.

But as the child grows older, a number of behavioral features develop that further complicate interpersonal and social adjustment. Among such features are

- Obstinancy
- Negativism
- Stubborness
- Bossiness
- Increased mood lability
- Bullying
- Low frustration tolerance
- Temper outbursts
- Low self-esteem
- Lack of response to discipline

In designing a treatment program, the clinician needs to consider ways of measuring and treating these secondary characteristics and complaints in addition to the treatment procedures directed toward the primary attention deficit.

85

Cumulative research evidence and work with ADD children and their families lead us to believe that the basic problems described in the Douglas model (chapter 2) are directly related to the social problems of these children. Children with poorly modulated arousal, difficulties in inhibiting responding, and problems in planning and controlling their behavior are highly likely to encounter at least as many difficulties in social problem-solving situations as in academic problem-solving situations. Consequently, treatment should address the cognitive, affective, and behavioral variables that appear related to social adjustment. One well-researched treatment approach that addresses these three variables is Interpersonal Cognitive Problem-Solving Training (ICPS).

TEACHING INTERPERSONAL COGNITIVE PROBLEM-SOLVING SKILLS (ICPS)

Our first attempts to alter the cognitive processes that regulate social skills of ADD children were guided by the work of Kanfer (1970, 1971), Kanfer and Karoly (1972), Spivak and Shure (1974), Shure and Spivak (1971, 1978) and Shure (1981). The three cognitive skill areas required for good self-control according to Kanfer and Karoly are self-monitoring, self-evaluation, and self-reward. Almost simultaneously, Spivak and Shure and their colleagues outlined the role of cognitive mediation in the development of interpersonal problem-solving skills in young children. Shure and Spivak described interpersonal cognitive problem-solving skills in terms of five distinct skills: problem sensitivity, alternative thinking, means–ends thinking, consequential thinking, and causal thinking. These ICPS skills are summarized briefly in the following paragraphs.

Skill Area #1

During the course of everyday social interchanges, a child needs to realize that problems can arise and be able to recognize them when they do. This skill area is called *problem sensitivity*.

Skill Area #2

The ability to generate varied solutions or alternatives when confronted with a problem is called *alternative thinking*. Alternative-thinking skills involve the capacity to brainstorm a course of options to solve social or interpersonal problems. The options must be feasible ones.

Skill Area #3

Means–ends thinking is the ability to conceptualize a strategy or to develop the step-by-step means that might be necessary to realize the solution to an interpersonal problem. (This includes recognizing potential goal obstacles the individual encounters.) The strategy developed must include a realistic appreciation of time. For example, waiting until one is bigger and stronger is not a realistic solution to an immediate problem in dealing with a bully.

Skill Area #4

The tendency to think of the probable consequences of alternative social actions with regard to oneself and others is called *consequential thinking*. Failure of impulsive children to consider and accurately predict the consequences of their actions is a central reason for the poor social adjustment of such children.

Skill Area #5

Causal thinking refers to the ability of the individual to appreciate personal and social motivations. This skill reflects an awareness that people's behavior is somewhat orderly and predictable and that interpersonal events are connected with past events. Such awareness helps one to better understand the meaning of the present.

Social Comprehension Ability

In aggregate, the five skill areas refer to *social comprehension ability*. Children who are deficient in such skills are likely to have social and interpersonal difficulties.

Evidence of the relationship between ICPS skills and social adjustment, pioneered by the investigations of Spivak, Shure, and their associates, has been examined through a number of studies in which attempts were made to teach social problem-solving skills to children (see reviews by Urbain & Kendall, 1980, and by Pellegrini & Urbain, 1985). Although the training content and methods show some variance, the guiding assumption regarding these training programs is that maladaptive cognitive processes play a primary role in producing psychosocial disorders. One instrument for assessing these cognitive processes is the Means–End Problem-Solving Test.

ASSESSING ICPS SKILLS

The Means–Ends Problem Solving Test (MEPS) (Shure & Spivak, 1972) measures the capacity of the child to articulate the step-by-step means just discussed to solve a particular social problem by recognition and appreciation of the obstacles he encounters and the necessary time framework anticipated to realize the problem resolution. The Children's MEPS Test consists of stories dealing with social problems such as making friends, getting even with another child, and being elected class leader. The child is presented with the beginning and ending of the story aloud and is asked to make up the middle part of the story. The child's means–ends thinking score is the sum of the number of means, obstacles, and specific time references mentioned when making up the stories.

In comparisons of 23 ADD children in our program with a group of 23 normal children, significant differences between the two groups' MEPS scores were found (Johnson, 1985). The differences were statistically significant, and they were also large enough to be of practical significance. The ADD children's mean score (number of means of obtaining the ends) was 2.86, with a standard deviation of 1.81, whereas the control group mean was 5.17, and the standard deviation was 2.87 ($t = -3.25$, $p < .001$). All MEPS stories were read by graduate students who were unaware of group membership. The interrater reliability between independent scorers was .91, $p < .001$.

SIMULATED ICPS PERFORMANCE OF ADD CHILDREN AND CONTROL GROUP CHILDREN

A frequent criticism of assessment in the area of ICPS is that a child's capacity to solve hypothetical problems is not necessarily related to real-life problem solving (Butler & Meichenbaum, 1981). Therefore, we conducted a study in which ADD children and a group of normal controls were presented with the following situation. Each child was escorted to an unoccupied room to be presented with the problem situation and interviewed individually by the experimenter. The problem the children faced involved a complimentary shirt provided for each child participating in the study; the experimenter told each child that when he counted the shirts, he discovered that there were only 22 shirts for 23 children. He also told each child that there was not sufficient time to reorder an additional shirt and that only ideas suggested by the children would be used to solve the problem, because the shirts belonged to the children. The experimenter then obtained each child's problem-solving responses.

These sessions were tape-recorded and later transcribed. An interrater reliability coefficient was computed on one-half of the children in both groups to determine how consistently the experimenter and a nonparticipating graduate student in psychology could identify the number of alternative problem-solving solutions generated. This coefficient was .95, $p<.001$. The child's score on the simulated problem was the sum of his alternative responses. This manner of scoring parallels earlier research that evaluated children's interpersonal problem-solving skills in simulated situations.

A one-tailed t-test analysis was used to determine the significance of the difference between the mean number of alternative solutions demonstrated by the ADD and the control groups in this simulated interpersonal problem situation. The results indicated that the ADD group performed significantly poorer than the control group in the simulated interpersonal problem situation ($t = -1.75$, $p<.04$).

Implications for Treatment

The findings that ADD children do score low on measures such as the MEPS and that performance on the MEPS is related to real-life problem solving suggest that ICPS training can be a useful means of improving the social skills of these children. Yet, there are at least two cautions to be observed before the implementation of such training. *First,* there was a good deal of variability among the ADD children on both the MEPS and the simulated problem. Some of the ADD children scored better than some of the normal children on both tasks. The clinician therefore should be certain that each child who receives ICPS training does in fact need such training. *Second,* the "real-life" problem involving the shirts was not an urgent one in that no time requirements were set. Even more important, the situation did not involve a high degree of emotional arousal and might therefore not be characteristic of the demands of many of the real-life situations in which the ADD child has difficulty. Though an ADD child might have good ICPS skills, he might not use them in situations where rapid decisions must be made and while in a state of high physiological arousal. One should be sensitive to these and other potential obstacles to success in the day-to-day conducting of ICPS skill-training sessions. For a discussion of the relationship between MEPS scores and real-life problem solving see Butler and Meichenbaum (1981).

CONDUCTING ICPS SESSIONS

In our program, we conduct the ICPS sessions in groups of four or five children. Although we model our approach after the one used by Shure and Spivak (1974, revised, 1978) in their 46-lesson curriculum for classroom teachers, we do not conduct our sessions in a sequential manner. A number of variables must be considered if such training is to have a lasting and meaningful effect upon the way in which children think about and deal with social problems. Among these variables are selection of target problems and problem situations, individual differences among children, and instructional format and sequence of activities.

ASSESSMENT SOURCES

Home Situations Questionnaire

One direct source of potential target problems is the Home Situations Questionnaire (chapter 4). If a child is rated, for example, as having severe problems when visitors are in the home and/or when he is in the supermarket, the clinician can query further about the nature of these problems, and, if it appears that ICPS skill deficits are involved, then simulated situations can be constructed for treatment that relate to these specific problems.

Self-Control Rating Scale (SCRS)

The Self-Control Rating Scale (chapter 4) contains items that often suggest good social skill target areas. Butting into games or activities and insisting on imposing one's own will rather than going along with the group are examples. Along with the SCRS, we also ask both parents and teachers to list five current problem areas they would most like the treatment to address.

A Taxonomy of Problematic Social Situations for Children (TOPS)

Kenneth Dodge and his colleagues at Indiana University have conducted a series of studies that have resulted in a Taxonomy of Problematic Social Situations for children (Dodge, McCluskey, & Feldman, 1985). Beginning with a large list of possible problem situations, Dodge and his colleagues asked elementary school teachers to identify from this list those situations that were actually problematic for children in their school. The resulting problems were then presented to a group of children identified by teachers and peers as either socially well adapted or socially rejected. The results of a factor analysis of these data revealed five clusters or factors that are typically problematic for socially rejected elementary children

1. Peer group entry (initiating entry and being excluded)
2. Response to provocation (preserving self-integrity while maintaining peer status)
3. Response to failure (dealing with being identified as inferior)
4. Social expectations (dealing with situations in which clear social norms exist)
5. Teacher expectations (dealing with situations in which clear teacher norms exist)

A study currently underway in our laboratory addresses the cognitive processes that guide the behavior of ADD children in each of these situations. This study utilizes a role-playing interview and scoring system also developed by Dodge and his colleagues. This interview is particularly well suited to our program because identification and modification of deficient and distorted cognition are central to the cognitive–behavioral form of treatment. Examples from this interview technique follow:

> *Situation #1:* Let's pretend we're outside at recess. You're playing tag, but all of a sudden you notice that I'm standing by myself. You come over to talk to me, and you see that I've been crying and there are tears in my eyes. What do you do or say?

The clinician makes every attempt to describe the situation vividly and with feeling in order to get the child to actually role-play the solution rather than simply relate to it as a hypothetical problem situation. The clinician then scores the child's response in terms of (a) whether or not the child appeared to actually be role-playing and (b) the competency of his response. The criteria for scoring the child's role playing are

> *A YES RATING:* The child answers as if the interviewer is another child. For example, "What are you crying about?" counts, as does an action such as actually walking toward the interviewer or touching her or him. A yes rating is also given if the child uses lots of expression in response, for example, if the child says "I'd say (shouts), YOU CAN HAVE IT."

> *A NO RATING:* A no rating is given for answers such as, "I would get a teacher." A no rating is also given for responses preceded by such remarks as, "I would say 'What's wrong?' " Answers after a prompt (Q) do not count as role-plays.

The criteria for scoring the competency of the child's responses are

> *Score 8:* Subject attempts to console the child or
> help the child personally. *Example:* "I
> would play with her." "I would hold you."
> *Score 6:* Subject asks the child what happened or if the child is all right.

Score 4: Subject tells, or offers to tell, someone in authority.
Score 2: There is no response.
Score 0: Subject laughs at the child. Subject does nothing. Subject didn't
know what to do or didn't answer.

0	2	4	6	8
		neither competent		
very incompetent	somewhat incompetent	nor incompetent	somewhat competent	very competent

The examiner is then instructed to rate the subject's response choosing
one of the numbers on the scale. Choosing a number between 4 and 6,
for example, is not allowed.

Other social-problem situations included in the Dodge interview are
listed in Fig. 6.1. In the actual interview, each situation is preceded by
the statement, "Let's pretend that. . . ." and followed by "What would
you do or say. . . ."

In applying Dodge's interview with individual ADD children, especially those who resist or react passively to the role-playing, incompe-
tent responses can be explored in some detail to help the clinician

FIGURE 6.1. Problem Situations from Dodge's Role-Playing Interview

I'm playing blocks with some of my friends after lunch. We're building a
really neat house. You come in the schoolroom and see us. Pretend that
you really want to play blocks with us.

We're in the lunchroom carrying our trays of food. I'm walking right be-
side you. I want to sit by my other friends. I accidentally bump you, and
you drop your whole tray on the floor. I look back at you.

The teacher has told the whole class to get in line for lunch. You are
standing in line. Then I come and cut in front of you. Let's pretend that I
say, "I'm standing here now."

I and some other kids have a new video game that we're playing with.
You can see that it looks like a lot of fun. We are taking turns playing
with it. You ask, "Can I have a turn?" Let's pretend that I say "No, you
have to wait until I say you can play."

I'm another girl in your class. You have some free time and want to talk
to someone. You see me sitting at my desk. Let's pretend that you decide
to talk to me.

FIGURE 6.1. (*continued*)

You're drawing with your crayons during free time. You are making a fire engine/butterfly. I am coloring too, but some of my crayons are lost. Let's pretend that I ask you, "Can I use your red crayon?"

We're in class now. The teacher is handing back arithmetic papers. When the teacher gives you your paper, you smile because you got all the answers correct. Then you notice that I missed six problems, and I am almost ready to cry.

Some boys/girls in your class have started a club. It's a real fun club, and we do some neat things. I'm in the club. Let's pretend that you wish to join the club too. One day you see me walking down the hall on my way to a club meeting.

When you get ready to go to school, your mother tells you that you can't leave unless you put on your rubber boots and your ugly black raincoat. When you get to school all the other kids have on shorts and tennis shoes. When I see you, I start laughing.

Your teacher has given you an assignment to write about reptiles. You don't even know what a reptile is or even how to spell the word. You notice me going right to the encyclopedia to start my report. You come over to see what's going on. You are really upset because you think you are going to get a really bad grade.

I brought my new soccer ball/Strawberry Shortcake doll to school. I let you play with it. Let's pretend that I said you could use it for the whole recess. Halfway through recess, I come over to you and say, "I want my ball/doll back right now."

We are in gym class. The teacher is having us run some races. I am really a fast runner and end up winning almost every race. At the end of class, the teacher says I will get to race against kids from other schools. You walk with me back to class.

You and I are playing checkers during the free time. I have three kings, and you don't have any. I am almost ready to jump your last man.

The whole class is working on a big picture to hang in the hall. The teacher is going to choose one person to be in charge and decide what we're going to draw in the picture. You would really like to be the person in charge. The teacher says to me, "(name), I'm going to let you be in charge here. What shall we draw?"

Reproduced by permission of the authors.

understand how the child thinks and reasons or fails to think about real-life problem situations.

Young ADD children and those with severe impulsivity are often quite poor at role-playing in both the evaluation exercises and the treatment sessions that follow. Reflectivity and perspective-taking skills could well be a necessary prerequisite for role enactment. In such cases, the clinician can still use the role-playing interview as a guide to or structured probe of the child's self-assessment of problem areas. In deciding which of several identified problems to begin with in treatment, an important consideration is the degree to which the child himself recognizes and accepts responsibility for a particular problem.

INDIVIDUAL DIFFERENCES
AMONG CHILDREN

Among differences that can affect response to training are the child's age, intelligence, expressive language ability, and attributional style.

Many ADD children have limited awareness of the fact that they are having social problems. Others might have a dim awareness but are unable to express what the problems are. Children with an external locus of control who believe that fate, luck, or chance determines their success or failure in day-to-day social interactions do not reflect much about the nature of such problems and are often not highly motivated to accept responsibility for them. "It's my brother who starts it," "Other kids are always bugging me," and "You should be talking to Ralph, not to me" typify many of the reactions we get when we attempt to describe a particular problem a child appears to have. As suggested above, and deserving reemphasis, it is much better to spend time probing for a problem that the child will accept responsibility for than to overwhelm the child with a host of problems.

INSTRUCTIONAL FORMAT AND
SEQUENCE OF ACTIVITIES

We stated earlier that our program does not follow the highly structured format others have used in providing ICPS skill training. We begin the social skills sessions only after some progress has been made in the academic problem-solving sessions (chapter 5), because newly gained academic expertise is readily rewarded in the clinic and school environments. Newly acquired social skills go unnoticed or are inconsistently reinforced by peers.

In approaching this complex and somewhat amorphous problem area, we have appreciated the clarification provided by Shure and Spivack, who have developed a system for helping children learn how to think about social problems. It is called *dialoguing*. Dialoguing refers to an interactive discussion between an adult and a child during which the five skill areas discussed earlier are taught. The five basic principles of dialoguing are

1. Both the child and adult must know the problem.
2. The child's solution must not always be viewed as the original problem. For example, if a child hits another child for teasing him, hitting is the child's solution and not the initial problem.
3. The problem must remain relevant to the child and not be altered to suit the adult.
4. The child, *not* the adult, must become engaged in and attempt to solve the problem.
5. The focus should be on *how* the child thinks, *not* on the specific conclusion he comes to.

A general characterization of the sequence we use once the target problems have been selected includes (a) clarifying the child's goals, (b) teaching impulse delay, (c) teaching the child to generate alternatives, (d) teaching consequential thinking, and (e) teaching children to recognize and deal with emotions. Each of these steps is discussed in turn.

Clarifying the Child's Goals

It is quite important here not to accept just any reasonable-sounding goal but to select a goal that will in fact be related to and guide actual behavior in solving this or similar problems. If, for example, the problem involves peer group entry, the assumed goal might be acceptance by others and admission to participation in enjoyable activities. In observing the child's behavior, however, it might become apparent that his actual guiding goals are disruption of the group, need for attention, desire for revenge on another child, or proof of superiority in the activity or game he is attempting to enter. Initial attempts to get the child to realize what he is actually trying to accomplish (his goals) in interactions with other children can be thwarted by the child's low level of cognitive awareness.

Renshaw and Asher (1983) described the process of goal construction as one that is often unconscious and that involves asking questions such as, "What's going on here?" and "What am I supposed to do?" When the goals of each participant in a social situation are fairly similar, social transactions progress smoothly; however, when one or more participants work toward a personal goal that is at variance with the group goal, dysfunctional social interaction results. Two vivid examples are given by Renshaw and Asher. One example involves two children playing a board game. The goals of the participants here might be to (a) win, (b) enhance or maintain relationships with each other, or (c) get better at the game. Even if the goal of a child is to win, he might cheat and attempt to dominate the game and undermine the possible prosocial benefits of the occasion in a number of ways.

The second example involves a new child at school. Here the child's goal could be to get attention quickly or to enter the new situation slowly and avoid being noticed. The new child who claims that he is really trying hard to make friends and is repeatedly rejected might, in reality, not be engaging in the types of strategies likely to achieve his goal. His strategies, rather, might be preconsciously intended to win at all costs. The task of the clinician then is to assess and help the child recognize and alter personal goals that put him in conflict with others.

The personal goals of ADD children have not been systematically studied, but one could expect that many of these children lack a sensitive awareness of their own goals in many social and interpersonal situations. As such, they would be unlikely to notice subtle or perhaps obvious differences between what they are working toward and hoping to gain from a social encounter and what another child or group of children might be seeking. This speculation is based on cumulative observations of ADD children who are often too energetically and egocentrically involved in the immediate present to engage in reflective examination of the subtle behavioral requirements for optimal social adjustment. Such examination could result in a more sensitive awareness of dissonant personal goals. Egocentricism as it relates to social role-taking skills has been extensively studied by Selman (1980) and Chandler (1973).

Teaching Impulse Delay

In several places in this book, differences between mediational and production deficiencies have been noted. Even if a child has no mediational deficiences such as poor ICPS skills, he might be unable to apply adequate social comprehension abilities because he has difficulty controlling the arousal and related impulsivity caused by the emotional intensity of real-life situations. Teaching children to react more slowly and with less intensity could require appropriate medication as an adjunct to cognitive training.

A study reported by Brown, Wynne, and Medenis (1985) compared the relative effectiveness of cognitive–behavioral treatment, methylphenidate, and a combination of the two. The cognitive–behavioral treatment involved 24 one-hour sessions in which verbal self-instruction training was combined with strategy training. The strategy training taught children how to break tasks down into component parts and how to use individualized yet generalizable problem-solving efforts on tasks of increasing difficulty. Children who received only the cognitive–behavioral training spent more time thinking about and formulating their responses on posttesting than did the medication-only group, who continued to respond as rapidly as before. The combined medication and cognitive–behavioral treatments, however, produced the most significant overall effects. The finding that cognitive training plus medication produces better results than either treatment in isolation (noted several years ago by Douglas et al., 1976) has important implications. For example, Keogh and Glover (1980) have stated that, although medication has been generally effective in reducing activity level, cognitive–behavioral forms of treatment have had more effect on problem-solving performance, decreasing impulsivity and increasing attention to tasks.

As a supplement to or in some cases as an alternative to medication, the clinician can also focus treatment specifically on the problem of impulse control by using relaxation-training procedures. Guidelines for the clinical application of relaxation procedures have been suggested by Meichenbaum (1985) in connection with stress inoculation training. These guidelines can, with some modifications, be applied to the treatment of ADD children. A guideline of particular importance concerns the need to make a connection during practice sessions between the relaxation procedures and the cues for identifying a potential problem situation outside the clinic. It is also necessary that the relaxation procedure be one that can be handily implemented in real-life problem situations.

Teaching the Child to Generate Alternatives

ADD children typically have difficulty generating more than one response to hypothetical problem situations presented during treatment. In a real-life confrontation, it is as if the ADD child's *thought* of verbal or physical retaliation occurs almost simultaneously with the *implementation* of the response. Shure and Spivack's research provides considerable support for the effectiveness of training children to think of multiple alternatives before responding to social and interpersonal problems.

As with the teaching of other cognitive skills, it is necessary to overcome resistance when conducting these sessions. ADD children often enjoy thinking of shocking responses and doggedly insisting that indeed that *is* what they would do. One 10-year-old boy, for example, responded to a discussion about what to do if someone makes fun of your pet dog by insisting with great feeling that, "I would secretly train the dog to attack and then sic him on every kid in the school." Such responses can be discouraged by establishing ground rules at the beginning of the session that stipulate that immature and unrealistic solutions do not count. The clinician can also use response–cost to reduce such answers. In such a situation, the clinician should avoid challenging the practicality or wisdom of an immature response. Usually the best response is to calmly say, "Yes, that is one thing, but what are some more reasonable things you could do?"

Teaching Consequential Thinking

The ability to think of reasonable alternative solutions involves what Spivack and Shure call *consequential thinking*. This requires the child to think through the sequence of events that would logically follow from each of the alternative solutions generated. This type of consequential thinking process requires sequential thinking as well as inhibition of impulsive thoughts and actions, two skill areas notably deficient in ADD children. Consequential thinking also involves perspective-taking skills. Perspective-taking requires a child to get outside himself and view the problem from another person's frame of reference.

As with the teaching of academic problem-solving skills, resistance to social skills training is often high, and progress is slow. There are no pat suggestions to overcome resistance. Each child represents a unique challenge. More important is clinician commitment and positiveness. ADD children do respond well to such training, as evidenced both by the improved quantity and quality of responses during treatment and by the ratings of parents and teachers that indicate improvement of social behavior following treatment.

As noted earlier, in order to encourage the real-life application of social skills training, it is necessary to organize treatment sessions around real-life problems drawn from the referral and assessment information, from parent and teacher input during treatment, and from the children's own selection of problem areas to work on. The reaction of individual children to the shift from hypothetical to real-life problems is both interesting and unpredictable. Some children react with an upsurge of interest and begin to respond more genuinely. Others, however, become quite emotional when the problems reflect their own actual and recent experience, and their involvement in the task decreases. Because establishing a correspondence between what is discussed in training and what takes place in the children's daily lives is crucial to the overall success of cognitive training, assisting the children in their understanding of and ability to deal with strong emotions is an important part of the treatment program.

Teaching Children to Recognize and Deal with Emotions

Cognitive training is often described in terms that lead one to think that cognition can be assessed, understood, and altered in a tidy and efficient manner. Changing a child's self-statements and altering the internal dialogue sound a bit like reprogramming a computer. In truth, of course, cognitions do not take place in an emotional vacuum but are related in complex ways to the child's feelings and behavior.

Wayne, a hefty 9-year-old boy we worked with recently, provides a good illustration of this complex interaction. We were attempting to teach Wayne to self-cue and relax when being teased or excluded from a group. In such situations, he would first become quite angry. Then he tried a steamroller tactic to make the others quit teasing and include him in. When that failed, he would become sad and aloof. The instructions that had been modeled for him several times were to delay for at least 1 minute before approaching another child or the group. During this delay Wayne was to take several fairly deep (but natural) breaths, and think of the words SMOOTH, CALM, QUIET, SOFT in a slow and drawn-out manner.

During a simulation exercise in which Wayne was asked to imagine and role-play a response to being teased, he would self-cue a relaxation response, as evidenced by his deep breathing and by his closed eyes. He did this for several seconds and then hesitated before responding. His response pattern, however, was similar to that noted in actual situations. He became angry and then sad. The clinician asked Wayne if he was thinking of the four relaxation words, and Wayne replied, spitting out the words "Smooth, calm, quiet, smooth, calm—I hate this dumb stuff. People telling me what to do and telling me what to think. Take it easy. Take it easy. That's what my mom and my teacher say. Well it ain't easy. It ain't fair either. Kids are always leaving me out—and—and. . . ." Wayne then began to sob.

In the discussion following the incident, Wayne was not able to describe the difference between his feeling of anger and his feeling of sadness, describing them both as bad feelings. He also failed to see how he could do anything about these bad feelings stating "they just happen to me." In teaching children such as Wayne to recognize and deal with emotions, we incorporate the 10 steps described by Bash and Camp (1986):

1. Identify the need for recognizing a particular emotion.
2. Show facial expressions that characterize emotion.
3. Label the emotion for the student.
4. Define the emotion.
5. Provide a personal example.
6. Restate the definition.
7. Show picture. What might have provoked the emotion?
8. Show different picture. What might have provoked the emotion?
9. What's something the person could say or do to lessen or intensify the emotion?
10. Follow up by using the emotion label during the session or by identifying the emotion in literature.

Bash and Camp have developed a script and picture program designed to teach children about the emotions of anxiety, pride, disappointment, jealousy, confidence, and embarrassment. In our program, as a powerful supplement to the 10 steps, we show the children videotapes of their emotional reactions. We then engage the children in discussions of these emotional reactions and the accompanying thoughts and feelings.

GUIDED PRACTICE IN SIMULATED PROBLEM SITUATIONS

Once children have begun to develop better ICPS skills and have some skills in recognizing their emotions and controlling the arousal level these emotions influence and are influenced by, the clinician can increase the chances that the child will actually use these new skills in real life by providing simulated practice and role-playing exercises.

It is essential that these practice sessions be viewed by the children as serious dress rehearsal for coping skills they will be expected to use each day. The children then report back to the clinician both successful and unsuccessful attempts to apply these new skills. This feedback is used to guide the content of future practice sessions and to allow opportunity for praising successful generalized application of specific coping skills.

SUMMARY

This chapter described a number of ways one can understand the social and interpersonal difficulties of an ADD child. This understanding provides the basis for teaching the child to have better self-regulation and self-control. To produce treatment efforts that are durable and that generalize beyond the clinic, the clinician needs to address the thoughts, feelings, and behaviors that precede, accompany, and follow the child's social encounters.

In conjuction with the teaching of social skills, the clinician should not leave it to chance that others will notice improvements in the child's behavior. It is important to inform parents, teachers, and siblings of the nature of the treatment the child is receiving. Then one can seek their assistance in prompting and rewarding skill practice as a potent means of promoting durable and generalized treatment effects. Evaluation of such effects is the subject of the next chapter.

Chapter 7

Durable and Generalized Effects of Cognitive– Behavioral Training

Chapters 3 and 4 described screening and different procedures for identification and evaluation of ADD children. Chapters 5 and 6 described and illustrated the manner in which cognitive–behavioral treatment addresses the academic and social problems that characterize ADD children. This chapter presents the results of a study evaluating the effectiveness of cognitive–behavioral treatment.*

A general impression one gets from reviewing studies that failed to demonstrate generalization (and even from some that were successful) is that lasting improvement was not well planned for or integrated into the treatment. The present study was designed to evaluate a cognitive–behavior modification (CBM) program explicitly designed to facilitate durable and generalized improvement in the behavior and learning styles of 6- to 12-year-old ADD children. Phase one of this study evaluated immediate effects of treatment. Phase two evaluated the children 1 year later.

PHASE ONE

Screening

A letter was sent to 36 elementary schools in or near Terre Haute, Indiana, describing the characteristics of ADD children and indicating that a summer remedial program would be available at Indiana State

---

*This chapter is an edited and corrected version of a paper presented to the American Psychological Association by Edward Kirby in August 1984.

University. Teachers were asked to discuss their potential referrals with the child's parent or guardian and to have them contact the university if they concurred with the teacher that the referral seemed appropriate.

If, after extended phone conversations between the senior author and the parent or guardian, a child appeared to fit the description of ADD provided in the *Diagnostic and Statistical Manual of Mental Disorders* (1980), screening continued. Hyperactivity rating scales (Conners, 1969) were mailed to the home and the school for parents and teachers to complete. If a child's score on either of these scales was 16 or higher, the *Daily Behavior Checklist* (DBC) developed by Prinz et al. (1981) was distributed to the teachers of the referred children, who were then requested to observe and rate each child for 5 days. The DBC is a list of 11 hyperactive and 11 aggressive behaviors. At the end of each day the teacher circled the behaviors that occurred that day. If, for the 5 days, more aggressive behaviors were circled than were hyperactive, then the child was not accepted into the program.

Assessment

The following measures were used to evaluate the treatment:

Wechsler Intelligence Scale for Children—Revised (WISC-R) (Wechsler, 1974)
Of particular interest on this measure was the freedom from distractibility (FD) quotient. FD is based on the combined subtest scores of coding, arithmetic, and digit span (Kaufman, 1979). Verbal and performance quotients were also analyzed.

Peabody Individual Achievement Test (PIAT) (Dunn & Markwardt, 1970)
This measure provides scores in mathematics, reading, spelling, general information, and overall total achievement score.

Matching Familiar Figures Test (MFF) (Kagan, 1966)
This test is described by Kagan as a measure of conceptual style or tempo and yields scores on latency (the time a child hesitates before responding) and errors.

Self-Control Rating Scale (SCRS) (Kendall & Wilcox, 1979)
The SCRS is a 33-item scale. Each of the 33 items is rated on a 7-point scale by parents or teachers. Ten of the items are descriptive of self-control, 13 are indicative of impulsivity, and 10 are descriptive of a combination of both self-control and impulsivity.

Continuous Performance Test (CPT) (Rosvold et al., 1956)

The CPT was originally developed as a measure of brain damage (Rosvold et al., 1956) but has been used as an experimental measure of vigilance of attention. It consists of a rewired digital clock that displays a single-digit number at 1-second intervals. The child is instructed to keep his attention on the clock face and to ring a buzzer when (and only when) a 0 is followed by a 1. The performance is scored for inclusive errors and omissions. Impulsivity (inclusive errors) usually means buzzing when the 0 appears without waiting for the 1 to appear. Children who do well on this type of task appear to be able to focus attention well but are often unable to attend selectively and productively to tasks requiring a high level of problem-solving skill.

Children's Embedded Figures Test (CEFT) (Karp & Konstadt, 1971)

The CEFT is described as a measure of cognitive style and has consistently been related to the construct of field dependence-independence.

Locus of Control Questionnaire (LC)

This scale was developed for this study in order to measure the extent to which children believe that they, rather than "fate" or "luck," can control their lives. The questionnaire consists of twenty yes-or-no questions such as "If I have a bad day there is nothing I can do to make it better." This measure is experimental, and no reliability or validity estimates are yet available.

All of these measures were administered by male and female graduate students who had completed at least one course in individual psychological assessment of children. These students were kept unaware of which children were designated for which treatment groups.

Conners Teacher and Parent Questionnaires

The teacher questionnaire contains 39 items, and the parent questionnaire contains 48 items. Each item is rated on a 0 to 3 scale. Only 10 of the items on each questionnaire are scored for hyperactivity.

Subjects

Approximately 70 children were involved in the initial referral and screening process. Of these, 35 were scheduled for the assessment phase. Many children were eliminated from consideration for the program because their behaviors, although fitting the ADD description, were of recent origin and appeared highly situational in nature. Other reasons for rejecting children from the program included previously diagnosed mental retardation, unwillingness by the parent or guardian to guarantee a child's regular attendance and participation in the program, serious problems in addition to ADD characteristics such as uncorrectable hearing or vision problems, and signs of severe emotional disturbance.

Of the 35 children selected for further evaluation, 2 did not appear for testing appointments. Twenty-three of the remaining 33 children were eventually enrolled in the treatment. The major attrition factor from the assessment was absence of evidence of serious inattention or impulsivity. Several of these unselected children would be described as poorly motivated in school situations but generally able to do well on educational tasks.

Method

Sixteen of the 23 children selected were randomly assigned to a CBM treatment group, and 7 children were assigned to a control group that received academic tutoring.* Two children dropped out of the CBM group, and one was unavailable for posttesting.

In addition to the CBM and control groups, a third group consisting of seven nonreferred children was evaluated using the screening and evaluation measures described earlier. These children were selected by the teachers of referred children in response to a request to select normally active but nonproblematic children. This group was used for descriptive comparison purposes only and was thus designated the *comparison group*. In the CBM group there were three girls, whereas the control and comparison groups included only one girl each.

CBM Treatment Sessions

The CBM treatment consisted of 2-hour sessions 4 days a week for 7 weeks. Each daily session was divided into three periods. During the first period, self-instructional training was provided using individual and group games as the teaching format. The objective was to have the children realize that, by using such self-instructional steps as (a) calming themselves down, (b) devising a reasonable strategy or plan, (c) monitoring their own behavior, and (d) keeping a check on impulsive tendencies, they could improve their chances for academic and social success.

---

*Following the 7-week treatment program, all control subjects were invited to participate in an after-school program offered in connection with the Indiana State University School Psychology Training Program. All control subjects were also invited to participate in the CBM treatment program to be offered the following summer.

Children were trained to self-instruct using the procedure steps described by Meichenbaum (1977):

1. The clinician models the solution of a task while talking to himself out loud (cognitive modeling).
2. The child performs the same task under the direction of the model's instructions (overt, external guidance).
3. The child performs the task while instructing himself aloud (overt self-guidance).
4. The child whispers the instructions to himself as he goes through the task (faded, overt, self-guidance).
5. The child performs the task while guiding his performance via inaudible or private speech (covert self-instruction).

The clinicians did not model self-instructions in a rote or strictly cognitive manner. Rather they were taught to be animated and responsive to the individual children. When, for example, it was noticed that a child was becoming frustrated and agitated or weary and defeated in response to a task demand, the clinician modeled self-coping statements such as "Boy this is hard. I've tried everything I can think of. I'm just no good at this kind of thing. Wait a minute. I'm getting all worked up. I can't do good work when I'm like this. I'll just calm down a bit and start again. That's better; now what can I do to get at this?"

The second period of the daily sessions involved using the self-instructional steps on more formal academic tasks such as reading for retention, mathematics, and learning to spell. The final period of each day was spent in group discussion and practice in the area of interpersonal skills. To help the ADD children deal more effectively with feelings of frustration, anger, and personal inadequacy, rap sessions or group discussions were conducted whereby the children could consider the potential value of "thinking before you act." Again, the self-instructional steps were employed as the means of improving interpersonal skills.

A number of manuals for therapists were provided to the clinicians (see Appendix). The main one used was by Padawer et al. (1980). However, manuals were not used in a rote fashion. They provided general treatment guidelines and gave treatment a degree of similarity across subjects. Children worked in small groups of four or five, with two clinicians assigned to each group.

A response–cost procedure was used to supplement the cognitive training, as described in the manual by Padawer and colleagues. Children were given 20 tokens before each session, and 1 of these was taken away each time a child engaged in inattentive and/or impulsive behaviors.

Staff Training

The authors' experiences are in agreement with those of Bash and Camp (1986), who report that people who are not thoroughly familiar with cognitive–behavioral theory do not readily learn to successfully implement cognitive–behavioral treatment. In this study, the clinicians who worked directly with the children were 10 advanced graduate students enrolled in school psychology and counseling psychology programs. Predominately doctoral candidates, these students met with the senior author for 2 hours a week for one full semester prior to working with the children. These preparation sessions included in-depth reading assignments, group brainstorming sessions while viewing and critiquing videotapes of previous CBM pilot programs conducted at Indiana State University, and development of age-appropriate training materials.

ASPECTS OF THE PROGRAM DESIGNED TO INCREASE DURABILITY AND GENERALIZATION

1. The selected children were told that this summer program had one main aim: to help them learn strategies and skills they could specifically use to improve their performance at home and at school. During the 7-week program, the children were frequently queried and reminded about applying their new CBM skills at home. In addition, discussions toward the end of the summer concerned anticipation of difficult situations that might arise in the school year ahead and ways to use their newly learned CBM skills in dealing with such situations.

2. The final 30 minutes of each daily session involved combining the children into larger groups of 10 to 12, to simulate a real classroom situation requiring standard individual seatwork assignments or group learning activities.

3. Adhered to each child's desk during the daily sessions were cue cards featuring a wide tortoise advising

CALM: Calm yourself down.
        *A*lways think of a plan first.
        *L*et your thoughts help your work.
        *M*ake sure you reward yourself.

In the fall, these cards were given to the subjects' teachers for similar individual desk reminders, to prompt the children to use their new skills and strategies back in the regular classroom.

4. During the last week of the 7-week summer program, classes were moved from the clinic to a local elementary school.

5. Children were given tee shirts depicting a tortoise traversing a maze. The slogan read "Succeed with Strategy." These shirts were worn 1 day a week during the program, and parents were urged to have their children wear the shirts at regular intervals during the normal school year.*

6. Prior to the beginning of the program, all the selected subjects' parents and/or guardians were invited to a meeting, for general information and explanations regarding the program. Parent involvement in treatment was also amplified throughout the program by an accessible library of cognitive training materials. Finally, parents were encouraged to observe training sessions (via one-way mirrors), to witness the sessions live, and/or to watch videotapes of the sessions.

Control Group Sessions

The self-instructional treatment group represented a multifaceted intervention, and the control group was designed to control only for certain features of the treatment, namely exposure to training material and trainer attention and involvement.

The control-group sessions were also divided into three periods involving (a) games, (b) academic tasks, and (c) discussions of interpersonal and social skills. The tokens available to the CBM subjects through the response–cost procedure were also available to this group. With the control group, however, tokens were not contingently connected to specific behaviors but were awarded on the basis of the clinician's evaluation of each child's overall performance each day. The academic materials such as work sheets and workbooks were generally the same or quite similar in the application of self-instructional training and response–cost system.

Children in the control group were also given "Succeed with Strategy" tee shirts and were taken to the local elementary school for the final week of the program. Parents of the control children were encouraged to observe, and suggestions were frequently given to parents of control-group children regarding discipline, homework, and such.

RESULTS

Table 7.1 summarizes the means, standard deviations, and F ratios of the three groups in the study. The table shows that the comparison group (nonreferred children) differed significantly from one or both of

---

*Clinician-"Coaches" also wore the tee shirts on designated days, and identification, camaraderie, and pride in being part of the program grew (visibly, though unmeasured).

Table (Means, Standard Deviations, and F Ratios) Comparing the Three Groups Prior to Treatment

Variables	1 CBM Group			2 Control Group			3 Comparison Group			F Ratio	P<	Source*
	N	$\bar{X}$	S.D.	N	$\bar{X}$	S.D.	N	$\bar{X}$	S.D.			
Conners Parent Symptom Questionnaire—Hyperactivity (PSQ)	11	19.6	5.3	6	19.5	3.0	7	3.4	4.1	27.4	.001	1 & 3 2 & 3
Self-Control Rating Scale—Parent Ratings (SCRS)	10	170.9	22.7	7	179.7	20.1	7	83.8	13.9	36.8	.001	1 & 3 2 & 3
Matching Familiar Figures Test—Latency (MFF)	13	14.7	12.7	7	12.9	9.0	7	13.3	7.1	.27	N.S.	
Matching Familiar Figures Test—Errors (MFF)	13	20.9	8.2	7	25.9	12.9	7	18.4	8.4	.96	N.S.	
Peabody Individual Achievement Test—Total Score (PIAT)	13	96.2	14.5	7	102.3	6.9	7	110.4	7.4	1.74	N.S.	
Freedom from Distractability (FD)	13	87.6	15.0	7	89.6	11.7	7	98.2	9.1	1.17	N.S.	
Children's Embedded Figures Test—Raw Score (CEFT)	13	11.8	5.0	7	14	6.4	7	22.5	.6	3.38	.05	1 & 3
Continuous Performance Test—Omissions (CPT)	12	1.2	2.2	7	.9	1.2	7	.25	.5	.90	N.S.	
Continuous Performance Test—Extraneous Errors (CPT)	12	11.5	10.5	7	1.0	9.9	7	1.0	1.2	6.04	.008	1 & 2 1 & 3
External Locus of Control (LC)	12	8.3	1.4	7	5.9	3.3	7	4.8	.8	6.7	.005	1 & 2 1 & 3
Conner's Teacher Rating Scale—Hyperactivity (TRS)	12	20.2	4.1	6	20.7	4.4	No data available for comparison group					
Self-Control Rating Scale—Teacher Ratings (SCRS)	10	165.9	21.6	5	171.8	10.6	No data available for comparison group					

*Multiple Range Test Duncan procedure for the .050 level.

109

the treatment groups on the PSQ, SCRS, CEFT, CPT (extraneous errors), and LC. The comparison group did not differ significantly on the MFF, PIAT (total score), FD, or CPT (omissions). The results of the Duncan Multiple Range Test, also reported in Table 7.1, show that the CBM group and the control group did differ significantly on 2 of the 12 measures.

To evaluate the overall effects of treatment, the gain scores of the CBM and control groups were compared, using a multivariate analysis of variance procedure or MANOVA (Huck, Cormier, & Bounds, 1974). All measures used in the study were included in this analysis, with the exception of the parent ratings that were excluded due to missing data. These measures were analyzed separately. The F ratio resulting from the MANOVA was 7.36, which, with 15 and 4 degrees of freedom, is significant at the .03 level of confidence.

Univariate F tests were computed to determine the individual contribution of each of the variables entered in the MANOVA. These results, summarized in Table 7.2, indicate that the CPT (omissions and extraneous errors) LC, and PIAT (mathematics) were the major contributors. CPT extraneous error scores and LC scores were significantly different at pretest. Analyses of the parent ratings indicate that the two groups differed significantly on the SCRS, $F = 9.48$, $p < .01$, but not on the PSQ, $F = 1.75$, $p < .56$. In terms of the direction of change, the CBM group showed improvement on all measures included in the study, with the exception of PIAT reading recognition and spelling subtests.

Table 7.2. Univariate F Tests of Gain Scores Immediately Following Treatment (DF = 1,18)

	F	Sig. of F <
Children's Embedded Figures Test (CEFT)	.80	.536
Continuous Performance Test (CPT)		
Omissions	4.16	.056
Extraneous Errors	6.94	.017
Matching Familiar Figures Test (MFF)		
Latency	.25	.626
Errors	1.00	.33
External Locus of Control (LC)	6.14	.023
Peabody Individual Achievement Test (PIAT)		
Math	14.77	.001
Reading Recognition	.39	.538
Spelling	.00	.991
General Information	.07	.793
Total Score	1.24	.829
Verbal IQ	.13	.72
Performance IQ	2.30	.146
Full scale IQ	.95	.342

The control group showed improvement on the PSQ, SCRS, CEFT, MFF, and PIAT General Information subtest. Tables 7.3 and 7.4 show the direction and magnitude of change for the two groups.

The early and continuing hypothesis of the proponents of CBM is that such an approach addresses the central difficulty of ADD children, which is their pervasive tendency to avoid developing and/or using cognitive mediation skills in a broad range of academic and social situations where such skills could greatly improve their adjustment. The finding that CBM does affect performance in a fairly broad range of academic and social areas offers additional support to this hypothesis. Although the findings of phase one of the present study are encouraging, the acid test for the contention that CBM can effect fundamental improvement in ADD children is the degree to which such improvements continue over time and occur in a variety of academic and social settings.

The second phase of this study involved a 1-year follow-up evaluation seeking to facilitate generalization and some long-term effectiveness of CBM training with ADD children.

PHASE TWO

Subjects

The second phase of this study involved booster sessions for one-half of the CBM subjects and a 1-year follow-up evaluation seeking to assess generalization and long-term effectiveness of CBM with ADD children. Of the 13 subjects who participated in the CBM group, 6 were randomly assigned to a booster-session group, and the remaining 7 were assigned to a no-booster-session control group. One of the booster-session subjects moved out of the district at midyear, leaving 5 booster and 7 no-booster subjects.

Procedure

Midway through the school year, immediately following phase one of the treatment, children in the booster-session group were visited in their school by a clinician from the summer CBM treatment program once each week for 8 weeks. The booster sessions consisted of review of self-instructional skills learned earlier and exploration of problem areas and situations where these skills could and should be applied. The clinicians also met with the children's regular teachers and explained the type of treatment that had been provided. Each child was asked to keep a self-monitoring checklist taped to his desk that listed such behaviors as

Table 7.3. Changes in Pretest and Posttest Scores for the CBM Group

Measure	Pretest Mean	S.D.	Posttest Mean	S.D.	Difference Mean	t value	p value <	N
Conners Parent Symptom Questionnaire—Hyperactivity/ (PSQ)	19.6	5.3	14.1	5.7	5.5	2.6	.025	11
Self-Control Rating Scale—Parent ratings (SCRS)	170.9	22.7	136.9	15.7	34	4.2	.002	10
Children's Embedded Figures Test (CEFT)	11.8	5.0	13.8	4.2	2.1	2.01	.068	13
Continuous Performance Test—Omission Errors (CPT)	1.2	2.2	.69	1.4	.53	1.02	.33	13
Continuous Performance Test—Extraneous Errors (CPT)	11.5	10.5	4.5	9.0	7	3.17	.008	13
Matching Familiar Figures Test—Latency (MFF)	14.7	12.7	18.5	10.4	3.8	-.93	.37	13
Matching Familiar Figures Test—Errors (MFF)	20.9	8.2	14.0	8.1	6.9	5.0	.001	13
External Locus of Control (LC)	8.3	1.4	7.0	1.9	1.3	1.9	.080	13
Peabody Individual Achievement Test (PIAT)	97.8	11.7	102.6	15.3	4.8	-2.4	.031	13
Math	97.4	12.1	102.3	15.9	4.8	-2.23	.047	12
Reading Recognition	95.2	13.6	94.5	15.3	.7	.45	.660	13
Reading Comprehension	97.5	14.7	101.0	13.1	3.5	-1.5	.153	13
Spelling	89.8	14.1	89.2	12.2	.6	.3	.810	13
General Information	99.7	16.1	101.3	13.7	1.6	-.9	.392	13
Total	96.2	14.5	97.2	14.1	1.0	-.30	.405	13
Wechsler Intelligence Scale for Children (WISC-R)								
Verbal IQ	101.6	20.6	102.6	17.6	1.0	-.30	.769	13
Performance IQ	100.4	9.1	110.7	14.0	10.3	-4.06	.002	13
Full Scale IQ	101.5	15.6	106.8	16.5	5.4	-2.45	.030	13
Freedom from Distractability Quotient (FD)	87.6	15.0	91.4	15.4	3.7	-1.31	.215	13

Table 7.4. Changes in Pretest and Posttest Scores for the Control Group

Measure	Pretest Mean	S.D.	Posttest Mean	S.D.	Difference Mean	t value	p value <	N
Conners Parent Symptom Questionnaire—Hyperactivity/ (PSQ)	19.5	3.0	16.7	4.9	2.8	1.3	.239	6
Self-Control Rating Scale—Parent Ratings (SCRS)	179.7	20.1	158.0	20.9	21.7	6.9	.001	7
Children's Embedded Figures Test (CEFT)	14.0	6.4	15.0	6.0	1.0	-.8	.474	7
Continuous Performance Test—Omission Errors (CPT)	.9	1.2	4.9	7.3	4.0	-1.4	.222	7
Continuous Performance Test—Extraneous Errors (CPT)	1.0	1.7	4.9	9.9	3.9	-1.0	.358	7
Matching Familiar Figures Test—Latency (MFF)	12.9	9.0	13.8	6.3	1.0	-.6	.555	7
Matching Familiar Figures Test—Errors (MFF)	25.9	12.9	23.0	12.2	2.9	.6	.590	7
External Locus of Control (LC)	5.9	3.3	7.7	3.4	1.9	1.5	.174	7
Peabody Individual Achievement Test (PIAT)								
Math	105.4	8.5	98.0	11.0	7.4	3.3	.017	7
Reading Recognition	106.0	6.6	103.9	5.1	2.1	1.7	.150	7
Reading Comprehension	107.1	9.7	100.0	10.2	7.1	1.8	.129	7
Spelling	97.6	7.6	97.0	7.9	.6	.3	.810	7
General Information	98.4	9.5	101.0	9.4	2.6	-.7	.501	7
Total	102.3	6.9	99.6	8.0	2.7	2.0	.093	7
Wechsler Intelligence Scale for Children (WISC-R)								
Verbal	104.2	11.4	102.3	11.2	1.8	.5	.638	6
Performance IQ	196.0	10.7	105.8	7.5	.2	.03	.977	6
Full Scale IQ	105.0	9.6	104.2	4.4	.8	.18	.863	6
Freedom from Distractability Quotient (FD)	89.6	11.7	87.0	13.2	2.6	.40	.701	7

- Did I focus in and understand the directions?
- Am I staying calm and keeping my mind on my work?
- Am I using a good strategy here?
- Am I getting anywhere, or am I stuck?

Children in the booster sessions were also given homework assignments that involved noticing and reporting each week the times when they used CBM-related skills in settings other than school.

Immediately following the 8 weeks of booster sessions, all subjects were reevaluated using an abbreviated battery of the measures used initially. Six of the subjects used as controls for the initial phase of the study were also reevaluated at this time. This testing occurred approximately 1 year after the treatment began.

RESULTS

The MANOVA procedure used to evaluate the effects of treatment in phase one of the study was also employed to evaluate the long-term treatment effects. With the CBM-booster and no-booster groups combined and compared with the control group, the F ratio failed to reach significance at the .05 level ($F = 2.93$, $p < 16$). The variables entered into the MANOVA were those listed in Table 7.5. Univariate F tests comparing the CBM-booster, CBM no-booster, and control groups indicated that only one measure was significant. This measure was the teacher ratings of hyperactivity ($F = 4.22$, $p < .03$). Teacher ratings on the SCRS came close to differentiating between the groups ($F = 3.56$, $p < .06$).

Table 7.5 presents means, standard deviations, and t values for the pretreatment and follow-up data for the combined CBM-booster and no-booster groups compared with the control group. The CBM group was found to improve significantly on six of the eight measures, whereas the control group showed a significant change on only one measure. This was the MFF, where the latency scores were found to decrease.

MANOVAs comparing the gain scores of the CBM-booster and no-booster groups indicated no significant differences between these two groups. Individual t tests of gain scores within each of these two groups showed that the CBM-booster group improved significantly on the TRS ($p < .05$), the PSQ ($p < .05$), and the SCRS mothers' ratings ($p < .05$). The no-booster group improved significantly on the TRS ($p < .008$) and on the FD measure ($p < .003$).

DISCUSSION

Overall, the results of the present study are consistent with other investigations of the potential clinical value of CBM in altering the behavior of ADD children (Bugental, Collins, Collins, & Chaney, 1978;

Table 7.5. Correlated *t* Tests Comparing the CBM and Control Groups' Pretreatment and 1-Year Follow-up Test Means

	CBM Group							Control Group						
	N	Pretest Mean	S.D.	Follow-up Mean	S.D.	*t* value	*p* value	N	Pretest Mean	S.D.	Follow-up Mean	S.D.	*t* value	*p* value
Conners Teacher Rating Scale —hyperactivity (TRS)	12	20.2	4.1	14.7	4.1	4.95	.001	6	20.7	4.4	20.7	4.7	0	1
Self-Control Rating Scale— Teacher Ratings (SCRS)	10	165.9	21.6	144.6	17.2	2.67	.025	5	171.8	10.6	186.2	13.3	−1.67	.10
Conners Parent Symptom Questionnaire hyperactivity (PSQ)	12	20.0	5.4	14.6	5.8	2.69	.025	6	19.0	3.0	17.5	4.0	.96	.20
Self-Control Rating Scale— Parent Ratings (SCRS)	12	168.6	22.6	155.3	25.8	2.13	.050	6	173.2	11.2	162.7	23.7	1.17	.15
Matching Familiar Figures Test (MFF) —Latency	12	12.5	6.7	11.3	6.0	.51	.35	6	13.4	9.8	7.4	5.0	2.5	.05
Matching Familiar Figures Test—Errors (MFF)	12	19.0	9.9	17.6	12.9	.50	.35	6	28.0	12.7	20.8	10.9	1.69	.10
Peabody Individual Achievement Test (PIAT)	10	96.8	14.3	101.7	17.3	−1.95	.05	6	103.3	6.9	103.3	9.8	0	1
Freedom from Distractability Quotient (FD)	11	90.8	15.0	102.4	16.1	−3.95	.005	6	89.7	12.8	97.8	8.5	−1.35	15

115

Douglas et al., 1976; Hinshaw et al., 1984; Konstantareas & Hermatidis, 1983). The number of children in each group was small and the variance within groups was fairly large, making it quite difficult to obtain statistical significance even though the gains of the CBM group were larger across several measures. The results encourage one to believe that CBM training can produce durable and generalized changes in ADD children; however, much more work is needed to support the claim that this is so. Although booster sessions did not appear to have much effect on the children, it is encouraging that, even without such sessions, gains are maintained over a 1-year period and are evident on a variety of measures.

The authors are optimistic about the potential value of CBM with ADD children but are humbled by several facts. The basic theoretical model for cognitive treatment is deceivingly straightforward and simple. Training children to alter long-standing and pervasive tendencies to avoid reflective self-guidance requires much more than the structural trappings of CBM. Teaching children to think is much more difficult than training them to talk about thinking. Moreover, even with a fairly large number of treatment hours intensively aimed at behavior change, the overall changes, although encouraging, remain relatively small.

Several years ago Karoly (1977) reviewed the literature concerned with developing self-control in children and concluded that such training has

1. Been conducted mainly in laboratory settings
2. Employed nonclinical populations
3. Neglected individual differences and cognitive–developmental variables
4. Failed to apply systematic pretreatment assessment
5. Operated under the assumption of a general skills deficiency (as opposed to possible perceptual, decisional, or motivational deficiencies)
6. Attempted to demonstrate the efficacy of a singular (or limited) intervention strategy
7. Focused on a narrow range of self-control responses, in which the frequent use of quotation marks around terms such as *hyperactive, impulsive, overactive, distractable, learning disabled, delinquent, excitable, aggressive,* and *disruptive* has served to absolve investigators of responsibility for delineating topographic boundaries and for blasting the patient homogeneity myth
8. Failed to pay sufficient attention to issues of maintenance and transfer

Although not all of Karoly's criticisms have been met, several of these shortcomings have been addressed by the present study. In attempting to bridge the gap between the precise but rather narrow findings of laboratory studies and the messier but more relevant application of self-management training with a clinical population such as ADD children, future researchers have their work cut out for them.

Chapter 8

Overall Summary and Concluding Remarks

The preceding pages have described our progress in understanding and treating attention deficit disorder in children. Initially, we focused on the directly observable characteristics of such children; however, it is now clear that the atypical and often baffling learning and behavioral styles of ADD children is rooted in the cognitions that mediate (or fail to mediate) academic and social behavior. Although the diagnostic term attention deficit disorder connotes a rather specific problem related to the initial focusing and maintenance of attention, this book has emphasized that, in fact, the difficulty is much more general in nature. ADD children not only have difficulty focusing attention on problems, they have difficulty recognizing the existence and nature of many problems, formulating a reasonable strategy for problem solution, remembering and sticking with a strategy once formulated, and evaluating the adequacy of a solution once attained.

Moreover, even when taught to carefully engage in the sequence of problem-solving steps, ADD children often fail to employ their new skills in real-life situations, resorting instead to previous impulsive behavior with little or no cognitive mediation. In view of these foregone considerations, conceptual clarity might well be gained by replacing the term *attention deficit disorder* with the term *self-regulatory difficulty*. The multicomponent treatment program we have developed is designed to impact on the thoughts, feelings, and behaviors that occur in situations requiring self-regulation.

Assessment instruments and procedures that relate to the thoughts and feelings that precede, accompany, and follow behavior during academic and social problem-solving are currently being developed and marketed at a rapidly escalating rate. We have described a number of

118

such measures that show promise of helping clinicians evaluate ADD children. Although the reliability and validity of many of these measures are not yet adequate for broad clinical use, progress is being made.

Our research findings, as well as others', concerning the efficacy of cognitive training are encouraging. The exciting promise of such treatment is that it encourages children to become aware of and take responsibility for directing and changing their *own* behavior. Also, in that treatment aims toward the development of cognitive events, processes, and structures, there is likelihood that more than a temporary prosthesis may result. Our own optimism for the potential value of the Indiana State University Cognitive Training Program is high; however, our optimism is tempered by the realization that we have not yet attained the goal of producing truly meaningful and durable changes that generalize to settings and problems outside of treatment.

An efficacious way of dealing with children who fail to respond well to treatment or who respond well during treatment but then relapse is to anticipate, discuss, and devise strategies for dealing with such occurrences. Children and their parents are taught to respond rationally and noncatastrophically to treatment failures and relapses. Clinicians likewise can benefit from such an approach. Specifically, one needs to acknowledge at the outset that ADD children present a formidable challenge; it will be easy, at times, to become frustrated at the maddening vacillation of ADD children—especially during the early phase of treatment. Don't catastrophize. Counsel yourself as we do: Cognitive training may, with enough time and effort, succeed in creating enduring new patterns of thoughts, feelings, and behaviors among ADD children, but it is not rational to expect this to happen rapidly, easily, or with all children.

References

Achenbach, T. M. (1978). The child behavior profile: I. Boys aged 6–11. *Journal of Consulting and Clinical Psychology, 46,* 478–488.

Ackerman, P. T., Dykman, R. A., & Peters, J. E. (1977). Teenage status of hyperactive and nonhyperactive learning disabled boys. *American Journal of Orthopsychiatry, 47,* 577–596.

Ain, M. (1980). *The effects of stimulus novelty on viewing and processing efficiency in hyperactive children.* Unpublished doctoral dissertation, McGill University, Montreal.

American Psychiatric Association. (1980). *Diagnostic and statistical manual of mental disorders* (3rd ed.). Washington, DC: Author.

Barkley, R. A. (1981). *Hyperactive children: A handbook for diagnosis and treatment.* New York: Guilford Press.

Barkley, R. (in press). Do as we say, not as we do: The problem of stimulus control and rule governed behavior in attention deficit disorder with hyperactivity. In L. M. Bloomingdale and J. M. Swanson (Eds.), *Attention deficit disorder: New directions in attentional and conduct disorders.* New York: Spectrum Publications.

Bash, M. A., & Camp, B. W. (1986). Teacher training in the think aloud classroom program. In G. Cartledge & J. F. Milburn (Eds.), *Teaching social skills to children* (2nd ed.). Elmsford, NY: Pergamon Press.

Beck, A. (1976). *Cognitive therapy and emotional disorders.* New York: International Universities Press.

Benezra, E. (1980). *Verbal and nonverbal memory in hyperactive, reading disabled, and normal children.* Unpublished doctoral dissertation, McGill University, Montreal.

Brown, A. L. (1975). The development of memory: Knowing, knowing about knowing, and knowing how to know. In H. W. Reese (Ed.), *Advances in child development and behavior, Vol. 10.* New York: Academic Press.

Brown, R., Wynne, M., & Medenis, R. (1985). Methylphenidate and cognitive therapy: A comparison of treatment approaches with hyperactive boys. *Journal of Abnormal Child Psychology, 13,* 69–88.

Bugental, D. B., Collins, S., Collins, L., & Chaney. (1978). Attributional and behavioral changes following two behavior management interventions with hyperactive boys: A follow-up study. *Child Development, 49,* 247–250.

Butler, L., & Meichenbaum, D. (1981). The assessment of interpersonal problem-solving skills. In P. C. Kendall & S. D. Hollon (Eds.), *Assessment strategies for cognitive-behavioral interventions.* New York: Academic Press.

120

Cairns, E., & Cammock, T. (1978). Development of a more reliable version of the Matching Familiar Figures Test. *Developmental Psychology, 14*(5), 555–560.

Campbell, S. B., Schleifer, M., Weiss, G., & Perlman, T. A. (1977). A two-year follow-up of hyperactive preschoolers. *American Journal of Orthopsychiatry, 47*, 149–162.

Chandler, M. (1973). Egocentrism and antisocial behavior: The assessment and training of social respective-taking skills. *Developmental Psychology, 9*, 326–332.

Conners, C. K. (1969). A teacher rating scale for use in drug studies with children. *American Journal of Psychiatry, 126*, 885–888.

Dodge, K. A., McCluskey, C. L., & Feldman, E. (1985). Situational approach to the assessment of social competence in children. *Journal of Consulting and Clinical Psychology, 53*(3), 344–353.

Douglas, V. (1980). Higher mental processes in hyperactive children: Implications for training. In R. Knights & D. Bakker (Eds.), *Treatment of hyperactive and learning disordered children*. Baltimore, MD: University Park Press.

Douglas, V. A. (1984). The psychological process implicated in ADD. In Lewis M. Bloomingdale (Ed.), *Attention deficit disorder: Diagnostic cognitive and therapeutic understanding* (p. 149). New York: Spectrum Publications.

Douglas, V. I. (1980). Treatment and training approaches to hyperactivity: Establishing internal control. In C. K. Whalen & B. Henker (Eds.), *Hyperactive children: The social psychology of identification and treatment*. New York: Academic Press.

Douglas, V. I., Parry, P., Marton, P., & Garson, C. (1976). Assessment of a cognitive training program for hyperactive children. *Journal of Abnormal Child Psychology, 4*, 389–410.

Douglas, V. I., & Peters, K. G. (1979). Toward a clearer definition of the attentional deficit of hyperactive children. In G. A. Hale & M. L. Lewis (Eds.), *Attention and cognitive development*. New York: Plenum.

Dulcan, M. (1985). The psychopharmacological treatment of children and adolescents with attention deficit disorder. *Psychiatric Annals, 15*, 69–86.

Dunn, L. M., & Markwardt, F. C. (1970). *Peabody Individual Achievement Test*. Circle Pines, MN: American Guidance Service.

Flavell, J., Beach, D., & Chinsky, J. (1966). Spontaneous verbal rehearsal in a memory task as a function of age. *Child Development, 37*, 283–299.

Flavell, J. H., & Wellman, H. M. (1977). Metamemory. In R. V. Kail & J. W. Hagen (Eds.), *Perspective on the development of memory and cognition*. Hillsdale, NJ: Lawrence Erlbaum Associates.

Garson, C. (1977). *Cognitive impulsivity in children and the effects of training*. Unpublished doctoral dissertation, McGill University, Montreal.

Gjerde, P. F., Block, J., & Block, J. H. (1985). Longitudinal consistency of Matching Familiar Figures Test performance from early childhood to preadolescence. *Developmental Psychology, 21*(2), 262–271.

Goyette, C. H., Conners, C. K., & Ulrich, R. F. (1978). Normative data on the revised Conners Parent and Teacher Rating Scales. *Journal of Abnormal Child Psychology, 6*, 221–236.

Henker, B., & Whalen, C. K. (1980). The many messages of medication: Hyperactive children's perceptions and attributions. In S. Salzinger, J. Antrobus, & J. Glick (Eds.), *The ecosystem of the sick child* (pp. 141–146). New York: Academic.

Hinshaw, S. P., Henker, B., & Whalen, C. (1984). Self-control in hyperactive boys in anger-inducing situations; Effects of cognitive–behavioral training and of methylphenidate. *Journal of Abnormal Child Psychology, 12*(1), 55–77.

Huck, J., Cormier, W., & Bounds, W. (1974). *Reading statistics and research*. New York: Harper & Row.

Jacobson, E. (1938). *Progressive relaxation*. Chicago: University of Chicago Press.

James, W. (1899). *Talks to teachers on psychology: And to students on some of life's ideals*. New York: Holt.

Jastak, J. F., & Jastak, S. (1978). *The Wide Range Achievement Test* (rev. ed.). Wilmington, DE: Jastak Associates.

Johnson, D. (1985). *Means–ends thinking and social problem-solving in attention deficit disordered and normal children*. Unpublished doctoral dissertation, Indiana State University, Terre Haute.

Kagan, J. (1966). Reflection–impulsivity: The generality and dynamics of conceptual tempo. *Journal of Abnormal Psychology, 71*(1), 17–24.

Kanfer, F. H. (1970). Self-regulation: Research, issues, and speculations. In C. Neuringer & J. L. Michael (Eds.), *Behavior modification in clinical psychology*. New York: Appleton-Century-Crofts.

Kanfer, F. H. (1971). The maintenance of behavior by self-generated stimuli and reinforcement. In A. Jacobs & L. B. Sachs (Eds.), *The psychology of private events*. New York: Academic Press.

Kanfer, F. H., & Karoly, P. (1972). Self-control: A behavioristic excursion into the lion's den. *Behavior Therapy, 3*, 398–416.

Karoly, P. (1977). Behavioral self-management in children: Concepts, methods, issues, and directions. In M. Hersen, R. Eisler, & P. Miller (Eds.), *Progress in behavior modification, Vol. 5*. New York: Academic Press.

Karp, S. A., & Konstadt N. (1971). *Children's Embedded Figures Test*. Palo Alto, CA: Consulting Psychologists Press.

Kaufman, A. S. (1979). *Intelligent testing with the WISC-R*. New York: John Wiley & Sons.

Kelly, G. (1955). *The psychology of personal constructs, Vols. I and II*. New York: W. W. Norton.

Kendall, P. C., & Braswell, L. (1985). *Cognitive–behavioral therapy for impulsive children*. New York: Guilford Press.

Kendall, P. C., & Finch, A. J., Jr. (1976). A cognitive–behavioral treatment of impulse control: A case study. *Journal of Consulting and Clinical Psychology, 44*, 852–857.

Kendall, P. C., & Finch, A. J., Jr. (1978). A cognitive–behavioral treatment for impulsivity: A group comparison study. *Journal of Consulting and Clinical Psychology, 46*, 110–118.

Kendall, P. C., & Wilcox, L. E. (1979). Self-control in children: Development of a rating scale. *Journal of Consulting and Clinical Psychology, 47*, 1020–1029.

Kendall, P. C., & Wilcox, L. E. (1980). A cognitive–behavioral treatment for impulsivity: Concrete versus conceptual training in non-self-controlled problem children. *Journal of Consulting and Clinical Psychology, 48*, 80–91.

Kendall, P. C., Zupan, B. A., & Braswell, L. (1981). Self-control in children: Further analyses of the Self-Control Rating Scale. *Behavior Therapy, 12*, 667–681.

Keogh, B., & Glover, A. (1980). The generality and durability of cognitive training effects. *Exceptional Education Quarterly, 1*, 75–82.

Kinsbourne, M. (1984). Beyond attention deficit: Search for the disorder in ADD. In L. M. Bloomingdale (Ed.), *Attention deficit disorder: Diagnostic, cognitive and therapeutic understanding*. New York: Spectrum Publications.

Kinsbourne, M., & Swanson, J. M. (1979). Developmental aspects of selective orientation. In G. A. Hale & M. Lewis (Eds.), *Attention and cognitive development*. New York: Plenum.

Kirby, E. A., & Horne, A. (1982). *A comparison of hyperactive and aggressive children*. Unpublished study.

Kneedler, R. D., & Hallahan, D. P. (1981). Self-monitoring of on-task behavior with learning-disabled children: Current studies and directions. *Exceptional Education Quarterly, 2*, 73–82.

Konstantareas, M. M., & Hermatidis, S. (1983). Effectiveness of cognitive mediation and behavior modification with hospitalized hyperactivies. *Canadian Journal of Psychiatry,* *28,* 462–470.

Kreutzer, M. A., Leonard, C., & Flavell, J. H. (1975). An interview study of children's knowledge about memory. *Monographs of the Society for Research in Child Development,* *40*(1, Serial No. 159).

Luria, A. (1959). The directive function of speech in development. *Word, 15,* 341–352.

Luria, A. (1982). *Language and cognition.* Silver Spring, MD: V. H. Winston & Sons.

Meichenbaum, D. (1977). *Cognitive–behavior modification: An integrative approach.* New York: Plenum.

Meichenbaum, D. (1985). *Stress inoculation training.* Elmsford, NY: Pergamon Press.

Meichenbaum, D. (in press). Cognitive–behavioral modification with hyperactive children. In L. Bloomingdale and J. Sergeant (Eds.), *Attentional deficit disorder.* New York: Spectrum Publications.

Meichenbaum, D., & Goodman, J. (1971). Training impulsive children to talk to themselves: A means of developing self-control. *Journal of Abnormal Psychology, 77,* 115–126.

Mendelson, W., Johnson, N., & Stewart, M. A. (1971). Hyperactive children as teenagers: A follow-up study. *Journal of Nervous Mental Disease, 153,* 273–279.

Meyers, A., & Craighead, E. (1984). *Cognitive–behavior therapy with children.* New York: Plenum Press.

Milich, R., Loney, J., & Landau, S. (1982). Independent dimensions of hyperactivity and aggression: A validation with playroom observation data. *Journal of Abnormal Psychology, 91,* 183.

Miller, P., & Bigi, L. (1979). The development of children's understanding and attention. *Merrill-Palmer Quarterly, 25*(4), 235–250.

Nowicki, S., & Strickland, B.R. (1973). A locus of control scale for children. *Journal of Consulting and Clinical Psychology, 40,* 148–154.

O'Leary, S. G., & Steen, P. L. (1982). Subcategorizing hyperactivity: The Stony Brook Scale. *Journal of Consulting and Clinical Psychology, 50,* 426.

Padawer, W. J., Zupan, B. A., & Kendall, P. C. (1980). *Developing self-control in children: A manual of cognitive–behavioral strategies.* Unpublished manuscript, University of Minnesota, Minneapolis.

Palkes, H., Stewart, M., & Freedman, J. (1972). Improvement in maze performance of hyperactive boys as a function of verbal training procedures. *Journal of Special Education, 5,* 237–342.

Palkes, H. S., Stewart, M., & Kahana, B. (1968). Porteus maze performance of hyperactive boys after training in self-directed verbal commands. *Child Development, 39,* 817–826.

Pelham, W. E. (1981). Attention deficits in hyperactive and learning-disabled children. *Exceptional Education Quarterly, 2*(3), 13–23.

Pelham, W. E., Atkins, M. S., Murphy, H. A., & White, K. S. (1981, November). *Operationalization and validation of attention deficit disorder.* Paper presented at the annual meeting of the Association for Advancement of Behavioral Therapy, Toronto, Canada.

Pellegrini, D. S., & Urbain, E. S. (1985). An evaluation of interpersonal cognitive problem solving training with children. *Journal of Child Psychology and Psychiatry, 26*(1), 17–41.

Posner, M., & Boies, S. (1971). Components of attention. *Psychological Review, 78,* 391–408.

Prinz, R. J., Connor, P. A., & Wilson, C. C. (1981). Hyperactive and aggressive behaviors in childhood: Intertwined dimensions. *Journal of Abnormal Psychology, 9,* 191.

Renshaw, P. D., & Asher, S. R. (1983). Children's goals and strategies for social interaction. *Merrill-Palmer Quarterly, 29*(3).

Robin, A. L., Fischel, J. E., & Brown, K. E. (1984). The measurement of self-control in children: Validation of the Self-Control Rating Scale. *Journal of Pediatric Psychology, 9,* 165–175.

Ross, D. M., & Ross, S. A. (1976). *Hyperactivity: Research, theory, action.* New York: John Wiley & Sons.

Rosvold, H. E., Mirsky, A. F., Sarason, I., Bransoume, E. D., & Beck, L. H. (1956). A continuous performance test of brain damage. *Journal of Consulting Psychology, 20,* 343–353.

Rotter, J. B. (1966). Generalized expectancies for internal versus external control of reinforcement. *Psychological Monographs, 30*(1).

Routh, D. K. (1980). Developmental and social aspects of hyperactivity. In C. K. Whalen & B. Henker (Eds.), *Hyperactive children: The social ecology of identification and treatment.* New York: Academic Press.

Rumble, S. (1985). *An examination of the psychological variables of attention deficit behavior in children.* Unpublished doctoral dissertation, Indiana State University, Terre Haute.

Rutter, M., Graham, P., & Yule, W. A. (1970). *A neuropsychiatric study in childhood.* Philadelphia: J. B. Lippincott.

Sarason, I. (1975). Anxiety and self-preoccupation. In I. Sarason & C. Spielberger (Eds.), *Stress and anxiety, Vol. 2.* Washington, DC: Hemisphere.

Sattler, J. M. (1982). *Assessment of children's intelligence and special abilities (2nd ed.).* Newton, MA: Allyn & Bacon.

Schleifer, M., Weiss, G., Cohen, N., Elman, M., Cvejic, H., & Kruger, E. (1975). Hyperactivity in preschoolers and the effect of methylphenidate. *American Journal of Orthopsychiatry, 45,* 38–50.

Selman, R. L. (1980). *The growth of interpersonal understanding: Developmental and clinical analyses.* New York: Academic Press.

Shure, M. B. (1981). Social competence as a problem-solving skill. In J. D. Wine & M. D. Smye (Eds.), *Social competence.* New York: Guilford Press.

Shure, M. B., & Spivack, G. (1971). *Solving interpersonal problems: A program for four-year-old nursery school children: Training script.* Philadelphia: Department of Mental Health Science, Hahnemann Medical College.

Shure, M. B., & Spivack, G. (1972). Means–end thinking, adjustment and social class among elementary school-aged children. *Journal of Consulting and Clinical Psychology, 38,* 348–353.

Shure, M. B., & Spivack, G. (1978). *Problem-solving techniques in childrearing.* San Francisco: Jossey-Bass.

Spivack, G., & Shure, M. B. (1974). *Social adjustment of young children: A cognitive approach to solving real-life problems.* San Francisco: Jossey-Bass.

Still, G. F. (1902). The Coulstonian Lectures on some abnormal physical conditions in children. *Lancet.*

Stokes, T., & Baer, D. (1977). An implicit technology of generalization. *Journal of Applied Behavior Analysis, 10,* 349–367.

Swanson, J. M., Nolan, P., & Pelham, M. (1985). Personal correspondence with Pelham.

Tant, J. L. (1978). *Problem solving in hyperactive and reading-disabled boys.* Unpublished doctoral dissertation, McGill University, Montreal.

Tant, J. L., & Douglas, V. I. (1982). Problem solving in hyperactive, normal, and reading disabled boys. *Journal of Abnormal Child Psychology, 10,* 285–306.

Urbain, E. S., & Kendall, P. C. (1980). Review of social–cognitive problem-solving interventions with children. *Psychological Bulletin, 88,* 109–143.

Victor, J. B., Halverson, C. F., & Montague, R. B. (1985). Between reflection–impulsivity and behavioral impulsivity in preschool children. *Developmental Psychology, 21*(1), 141–148.

Vygotsky, L. (1962). *Thought and language.* New York: John Wiley.

Wechsler, D. W. (1974). *Manual for the Wechsler Intelligence Scale for Children—Revised.* New York: Psychological Corporation.

Wender, P. (1971). *Minimal brain dysfunction in children.* New York: John Wiley.

Wender, P. H. (1973). Some speculations concerning a possible biochemical basis of minimal brain dysfunction. *Annals of the New York Academy of Sciences, 205,* 18–28.

Whalen, C. K., & Henker, B. (1976). Psychostimulants and children: A review and analysis. *Psychological Bulletin, 83,* 1113–1130.

Whalen, C. K., & Henker, B. (Eds.). (1980). *Hyperactive children: The social ecology of identification and treatment.* New York: Academic Press.

Whalen, C., & Henker, B. (in press). The social worlds of hyperactive (ADD-H) children. *Clinical Psychology Review.*

Wright, J. C. (1973). *The KRISP: A technical report.* Unpublished manuscript.

Appendix: Manuals for Therapists

Developing Self-Control in Children: A Manual of Cognitive-Behavior Strategies by Phillip Kendal et al. (unpublished). University of Minnesota.

Think Aloud—Increasing Social and Cognitive Skills: A Problem-Solving Program for Children by Bonnie W. Camp and Mary Ann S. Bash. Champaign, IL: Research Press, 1981.

Social Problem-Solving Curriculum for Enhancing Critical Thinking Skills. Middle Elementary Level by M. Elias and J. Clabby (unpublished). NJ: Rutgers University, 1981.

Star Training Program: Self-Control Training Program by S. P. Hinshaw, S. Alkers, C. K. Whalen, and B. Henker (unpublished). UCLA, 1980.

Understanding and Helping Hyperactive Children: A Manual for Parents and Teachers by Edward A. Kirby (unpublished). Indiana State University, 1980.

Author Index

Subject Index

About the Authors

Dr. Edward Kirby received his graduate training at the University of Illinois and Southern Illinois University. He has conducted research, provided treatment, and consulted in a variety of settings, including schools, camps, hospitals, mental health centers, and private practice. Dr. Kirby has presented workshops and papers at numerous regional, state, and national meetings. He is a past president of the school psychology division of the Indiana Psychological Association. Dr. Kirby is currently professor of Educational and School Psychology at Indiana State University in Terre Haute and director of the Cognitive Training Research and Treatment Program.

Dr. Liam K. Grimley is an internationally known school psychologist who is fluent in several languages. He holds five graduate degrees from European and American universities, including a PhD in school psychology from Kent State University. He served for 6 years as chairman of the Department of Special Education, School Psychology, and Communication Disorders at Indiana State University, where he is currently professor of Educational and School Psychology and director of Training Programs in School Psychology. He has had invited teaching assignments at Harvard University, the Sorbonne, and the National University of Ireland. From 1975 to 1978 he was editor of *The School Psychology Digest* (now *School Psychology Review*), the quarterly professional journal of the National Association of School Psychologists. He has published numerous articles, and, in 1985, was editor of the monograph entitled *Historical Perspectives on School Psychology*. He is coauthor of *Growing Up*, a publication for parents of school-age children and is contributing editor of *Growing Child,* the monthly newsletter for parents of young children. He has been the recipient of many awards, including the Presidential Award of the National Association of School Psychologists for promoting excellence in professional publications.